ALASKA CRUISE TRAVEL GUIDE

2024 Edition

Alaska Unveiled: "Embark on a Journey of a Lifetime as You Cruise through Alaska's Breathtaking Glaciers and Fjords"

by

Williams Carter

Copyright©2023 Williams Carter

All Right Reserved

TABLE OF CONTENT

IMPORTANT NOTE BEFORE READING _____ 5

CHAPTER ONE _____ 6

Introduction _____ 6
1.1 Welcome to Alaska: A Brief Overview _____ 6
1.2 Why Choose an Alaska Cruise? _____ 18

CHAPTER TWO _____ 24

Planning Your Alaska Cruise _____ 24
2.1 Selecting the Right Cruise Line and Ship _____ 24
2.2 Best Time to Visit Alaska _____ 37
2.3 Choosing the Perfect Itinerary _____ 48
2.4 Essential Travel Documents and Requirements _____ 59
2.5 Packing Tips for an Alaska Cruise _____ 70

CHAPTER THREE _____ 82

Embarking on Your Alaskan Adventure _____ 82
3.1 Port of Departure: Getting Started _____ 82
3.2 Life on Board: Ship Facilities and Amenities _____ 89
3.3 Safety Guidelines and Onboard Etiquette _____ 100

CHAPTER FOUR _____ 112

Exploring Alaska's Coastal Towns _____ 112
4.1 Juneau: Capital City and Gateway to Glaciers _____ 112
4.2 Skagway: Gold Rush History and Outdoor Adventures _____ 116
4.3 Ketchikan: Native American Heritage and Wilderness Excursions __ 120
4.4 Sitka: Russian Influence and Stunning Wildlife _____ 123

CHAPTER FIVE _____ 130

Cruising Alaska's Magnificent Glaciers _____ 130
5.1 Glacier Bay National Park: A Natural Wonder _____ 130
5.2 Hubbard Glacier: Witnessing the Power of Ice _____ 136

5.3 Tracy Arm Fjord: Pristine Beauty and Wildlife Encounters _____ 139

CHAPTER SIX _____ 144

Wildlife and Nature Encounters _____ 144
6.1 Whale Watching: Spotting Majestic Marine Life_____ 144
6.2 Bear Watching: Observing Alaska's Iconic Predators _____ 148
6.3 Birdwatching: Discovering Avian Diversity _____ 155
6.4 Exploring Alaska's National Parks and Reserves _____ 160

CHAPTER SEVEN _____ 166

Cultural Highlights of Alaska _____ 166
7.1 Indigenous Cultures: Learning about Alaska's Native Peoples ____ 166
7.2 Totem Poles: Artistic Expressions of Native Heritage _____ 177
7.3 Alaskan Cuisine: Seafood Delights and Local Flavors _____ 187

CHAPTER EIGHT _____ 204

Shore Excursions and Activities _____ 204
8.1 Kayaking and Canoeing Adventures _____ 204
8.2 Hiking and Helicopter Tours _____ 212
8.3 Fishing Trips and Crabbing Excursions_____ 216
8.4 Dog Sledding and Glacier Trekking _____ 220

CHAPTER NINE _____ 226

Tips for Maximizing Your Alaska Cruise Experience _____ 226
9.1 Capturing the Perfect Photos and Videos _____ 226
9.2 Onboard Entertainment and Enrichment Programs _____ 230
9.3 Souvenir Shopping and Local Crafts _____ 234
9.4 Best Practices for Responsible Travel in Alaska _____ 237

CHAPTER TEN _____ 241

Conclusion _____ 241
10.1 Appendix: Basic Phrases and Vocabulary _____ 241

IMPORTANT NOTE BEFORE READING

You might find a special trip experience in these pages.

The purpose of this Alaska cruise travel guide is to inspire your creativity, imagination, and sense of adventure. Since we think that the beauty of every discovery should be experienced firsthand, free from visual filter and prejudices, you won't find any pictures here. Every monument, every location, and every secret nook are waiting for you when you get there, eager to surprise and amaze you. Why should we ruin the wonder and excitement of the initial impression? Prepare to set off on a voyage where your imagination will serve as both your single mode of transportation and your personal tour guide. Keep in mind that your own creations are the most attractive.

This book lacks a map and photographs, in contrast to many other manuals. Why? Because in our opinion the best discoveries are made when a person gets lost, lets themselves go with the flow of the environment, and embraces the ambiguity of the road.

Be cautious, trust your gut, and expect the unexpected. In a world without maps, where roads are made with each step you take, the magic of the voyage starts now.

CHAPTER ONE

Introduction

1.1 Welcome to Alaska: A Brief Overview

Alaska, known as "The Last Frontier," captivates the imagination with its awe-inspiring landscapes, untouched wilderness, and remarkable natural wonders. Situated in the far northwestern corner of North America, this expansive state is renowned for its breathtaking beauty, diverse wildlife, and vibrant indigenous cultures. Embarking on an Alaska cruise adventure opens the door to a world of towering glaciers, majestic mountains, pristine fjords, and abundant wildlife.

Geography of Alaska:

Alaska's geography is a testament to nature's grandeur and diversity. Spanning over 663,000 square miles (1.7 million square kilometers), it holds the distinction of being the largest state in the United States. This vast expanse encompasses a remarkable variety of landscapes, from its awe-inspiring coastline to its majestic interior.

Alaska's coastline stretches for approximately 6,640 miles (10,686 kilometers), tracing a meandering path along the Pacific Ocean and the Bering Sea. Along this rugged and dramatic shoreline, you'll encounter towering cliffs that plunge into the sea, picturesque bays that provide shelter for marine life, and mesmerizing fjords carved by ancient glaciers. The sight of these rugged coastal formations, often cloaked in mist and touched by the bracing sea breeze, is a testament to the raw power and beauty of nature.

Venturing inland, Alaska's interior reveals a pristine wilderness of unparalleled beauty. This vast region is a tapestry of contrasting landscapes, where snow-capped mountains, rolling tundra, and expansive forests converge. Alaska is home to 17 of the country's 20 highest peaks, including the iconic Denali, formerly known as Mount McKinley. Denali towers majestically at an impressive height of 20,310 feet (6,190 meters), making it the tallest mountain in North America. Its summit is often shrouded in a crown of clouds, creating an ethereal and otherworldly presence that captivates all who lay eyes upon it.

The interior of Alaska is characterized by its vast expanses of untamed wilderness. Here, you'll find expansive national parks, such as Denali National Park and Preserve, Wrangell-St. Elias National Park and Preserve, and Gates of the Arctic National Park and Preserve. These protected areas encompass millions of acres, serving as havens for a rich array of wildlife, including grizzly bears, wolves, moose, caribou, and Dall sheep. As you explore these pristine landscapes, you'll witness the raw power of nature and the delicate balance of its ecosystems.

Alaska's geography is also shaped by its glaciers, which have sculpted the land over thousands of years. Glaciers, vast rivers of ice, can be found throughout the state, including in famous locations like Glacier Bay National Park and Preserve and Kenai Fjords National Park. These frozen giants showcase nature's artistry, with towering ice walls, ethereal blue hues, and the constant movement of calving ice. Witnessing a glacier in person is a humbling experience, reminding us of the forces that have shaped the land and continue to shape it today.

Glaciers of Alaska:

Alaska's glaciers are a testament to the immense power and beauty of nature. These colossal bodies of ice have shaped the landscape of the state over millions of years, leaving behind a legacy of breathtaking vistas and awe-inspiring displays.

Glaciers can be found throughout Alaska, but some of the most renowned locations to witness their splendor are Glacier Bay National Park and Preserve, Kenai Fjords National Park, and Wrangell-St. Elias National Park. These protected areas offer visitors a front-row seat to the majesty of these frozen giants and provide a glimpse into the ancient processes that have shaped the land.

Glacier Bay National Park and Preserve, located in southeastern Alaska, is a UNESCO World Heritage site and a true gem of the state. The park boasts over 3.3 million acres (1.3 million hectares) of pristine wilderness, where massive tidewater glaciers flow into the bay. Witnessing the monumental scale of these glaciers is an awe-inspiring experience. As you sail through the bay, you'll marvel at the ever-changing hues of blue radiating from the ice, ranging from a translucent turquoise to a deep sapphire. The sight of these immense rivers of ice meeting the sea is humbling, reminding us of the continuous cycle of creation and destruction in the natural world.

Kenai Fjords National Park, located on the Kenai Peninsula, is another remarkable destination for glacier enthusiasts. The park is home to numerous tidewater glaciers, including the famous Exit Glacier. As you hike along the trails, you'll be treated to breathtaking views of the glaciers as they flow down from the Harding Icefield, a vast expanse of ice covering over 300 square miles (777 square kilometers). Witnessing the stark contrast between the icy blue of the glaciers and the surrounding verdant forests is a sight that will stay with you forever.

Wrangell-St. Elias National Park, the largest national park in the United States, offers visitors an opportunity to explore a vast and wild landscape shaped by glaciers. The park is home to some of the most massive glaciers in Alaska, including the Malaspina Glacier, which covers an area larger than the state of Rhode Island. The sheer magnitude of these glaciers is awe-inspiring, stretching as far as the eye can see and reminding us of the incredible forces at work in shaping the Earth's surface.

When you stand before a glacier in Alaska, you become acutely aware of its dynamic nature. The crackling and booming sounds that fill the air are a testament to the constant movement and transformation of these frozen giants. Witnessing the calving of ice, where massive chunks break off and crash into the sea, is a thrilling and humbling experience. The chill in the air serves as a reminder of the icy world you are immersed in, as you bear witness to the ever-changing landscape shaped by these powerful natural forces.

In summary, Alaska's glaciers are a sight to behold. They are not only majestic in their scale and beauty but also serve as a powerful reminder of the Earth's geological processes and the delicate balance of our planet's ecosystems. Witnessing the incredible hues of blue, hearing the sounds of cracking ice, and feeling the chill in the air is a profound experience that connects us to the natural world in a deeply meaningful way. Alaska's glaciers are a testament to the power and majesty of nature, and they beckon us to explore and protect the fragile wonders of our planet.

Denali National Park:

Nestled in the heart of Alaska, Denali National Park and Preserve stands as a crown jewel of the state, inviting visitors to immerse themselves in pristine wilderness and witness the wonders of nature on a grand scale. Encompassing over six million acres (2.4 million hectares), this vast expanse of protected land is a sanctuary for both wildlife and those seeking an unparalleled adventure.

The centerpiece of Denali National Park is Denali itself, formerly known as Mount McKinley. Rising to a staggering height of 20,310 feet (6,190 meters), Denali is the tallest mountain in North America, commanding the landscape with its snow-clad peaks. The mountain's native name, Denali, means "the high one" or "the great one," and it is a name that befits its majestic presence. As you venture into the park, the sight of this awe-inspiring mountain will leave you in awe, a testament to the grandeur and power of nature.

Denali National Park is much more than just a mountain. Its diverse ecosystems encompass a range of landscapes, from vast taiga forests to expansive tundra. The park is a mosaic of ecosystems, each offering its unique beauty and serving as a vital habitat for a wide variety of wildlife species. Exploring Denali's untamed landscapes presents an opportunity to encounter some of Alaska's most iconic animals in their natural habitat.

The park is renowned for its populations of grizzly bears, which roam the wilderness in search of food and mates. Catching a glimpse of these magnificent creatures as they forage or fish in the park's rivers is a thrilling and humbling experience. Moose, with their towering antlers, can also be spotted in the park's marshy areas, gracefully navigating the wetlands. Wolves, known for their elusive nature, patrol the park's boundaries, leaving behind tracks that tell tales of their presence.

Among the wildlife that calls Denali National Park home, Dall sheep are a sight to behold. These agile and sure-footed animals navigate the rugged slopes of the mountains, displaying their majestic white coats against the dramatic backdrop of the landscape. As you witness these elegant creatures in their natural environment, you gain a profound appreciation for the resilience and adaptability of wildlife in Alaska's untamed wilderness.

Exploring Denali National Park goes beyond encounters with wildlife. The park offers a range of outdoor activities, including hiking, backpacking, and mountaineering, allowing visitors to immerse themselves in the vastness of the wilderness. Trails wind through valleys, offering breathtaking vistas of meandering rivers, alpine meadows adorned with vibrant wildflowers, and glaciers that carve their way down from the towering peaks. The sense of solitude and connection to nature found within the park's boundaries is unparalleled.

In summary, Denali National Park and Preserve stands as a testament to the wild beauty of Alaska. Its towering mountains, pristine wilderness, and diverse ecosystems provide a sanctuary for wildlife and a playground for adventurers. Witnessing the majesty of Denali, encountering its iconic wildlife, and exploring its untamed landscapes is a highlight of any Alaska cruise. Denali National Park offers a glimpse into the raw power and beauty of nature, reminding us of the need to preserve and protect these treasures for future generations to enjoy.

Native Alaskan Cultures:

Alaska's cultural heritage is a tapestry woven with the vibrant threads of its native peoples. The state is a mosaic of diverse indigenous groups, each with its unique languages, art forms, and spiritual traditions. Exploring the rich cultural heritage of Alaska's native communities offers a profound glimpse into the region's history, wisdom, and enduring connection to the land.

Alaska is home to a multitude of indigenous groups, including the Iñupiat, Yupik, Aleut, Tlingit, Haida, Athabascan, and many more. These communities have inhabited the land for thousands of years, developing distinct ways of life that are deeply intertwined with the natural world. As you delve into the cultural tapestry of Alaska, you'll discover a rich tapestry of traditions, stories, and practices that have been passed down through generations.

One of the most iconic and recognizable symbols of Alaska's native cultures is the totem pole. These intricately carved wooden structures serve as more than mere decorations; they are powerful storytelling mediums that convey ancestral narratives, legends, and spiritual beliefs. Totem poles can be found in various Alaskan towns, proudly standing as testaments to the artistic expressions and cultural heritage of indigenous communities. Each totem pole is a unique work of art, with its own distinct symbolism, animal motifs, and clan crests, reflecting the identity and history of the tribe or community that created it. Standing before a totem pole, you can feel the spirits of the past come alive, whispering their stories and teachings to those willing to listen.

In addition to totem poles, Alaska's native communities express their cultural heritage through a rich array of art forms, including intricate beadwork, basket weaving, mask carving, and storytelling. These artistic traditions are not just expressions of creativity; they are windows into the collective memory and soul of the indigenous peoples of Alaska. Each artwork carries within it a story, a connection to the land, and a celebration of the natural world. The colors, patterns, and symbols used in these art forms often carry deep spiritual and cultural significance, encapsulating the values, traditions, and identity of the native communities.

Exploring Alaska's native cultural heritage also offers the opportunity to engage with the living traditions of these communities. Cultural events, such as powwows, potlatches, and traditional dances, provide a firsthand experience of the vibrant traditions and contemporary expressions of Alaska's indigenous cultures. These gatherings bring together people from various tribes, allowing for the sharing of stories, songs, dances, and food, fostering a sense of community, unity, and cultural resilience.

By embracing the cultural heritage of Alaska's native peoples, visitors can develop a deeper appreciation for the interconnectedness of all life and gain insights into sustainable living practices, deep spiritual connections, and profound respect for the land. The wisdom, resilience, and creativity of these communities serve as a source of inspiration and a reminder of the profound knowledge and harmony that can be found in indigenous cultures.

In summary, Alaska's native cultural heritage is a treasure trove of traditions, stories, and art forms that provide a deeper understanding of the region's history, spirituality, and connection to the land. The totem poles, intricate artworks, and vibrant cultural events serve as gateways into the rich tapestry of indigenous cultures, allowing visitors to appreciate the wisdom, resilience, and creativity of Alaska's native communities. Exploring the cultural heritage of Alaska is an invitation to embrace diversity, cultivate respect, and honor the ancient traditions that have shaped this magnificent land.

Alaska's Wildlife:

Embarking on an Alaska cruise opens the door to a world teeming with diverse and magnificent wildlife. The state's vast and unspoiled wilderness, both on land and in the sea, offers a sanctuary for an array of fascinating creatures. From soaring birds to playful sea otters and from charismatic sea lions to the gentle giants of the ocean, the wildlife encounters that await you in Alaska are nothing short of awe-inspiring.

Alaska's skies are adorned with the regal presence of bald eagles, symbolizing freedom and strength. These majestic birds, with their impressive wingspans and piercing eyes, are a common sight along the coast and in the inland areas. As you glide through the Alaskan waters, keep a watchful eye on the skies above, as you might witness the breathtaking sight of an eagle swooping down to catch its prey or perching on a tree branch, surveying its domain.

Another avian marvel that captures the hearts of visitors is the puffin. These charming seabirds, with their colorful beaks and comical waddling on land, inhabit Alaska's coastal regions. Their ability to dive deep into the ocean in search of fish and their distinctive appearance make them a beloved sight for nature enthusiasts. Spotting a puffin bobbing on the waves or witnessing a group of them taking flight in unison is a delightful spectacle that epitomizes the wonders of Alaska's wildlife.

Alaska's coastal waters are a haven for marine life, attracting a multitude of species that thrive in its nutrient-rich currents. Sea lions, with their playful antics and boisterous roars, can often be seen basking on rocky outcrops or swimming gracefully in groups. Their social dynamics and impressive agility in the water make them a captivating sight to behold.

The charming sea otter, a keystone species in Alaska's marine ecosystems, is a true ambassador of the state's coastal beauty. These endearing creatures can be observed floating on their backs, using rocks as tools to crack open shells and feast on their favorite prey. Their adorable faces and playful behavior make them beloved icons of Alaska's wildlife, and encountering them in their natural habitat is an experience filled with joy and admiration.

However, perhaps the pinnacle of wildlife encounters on an Alaska cruise is the opportunity to witness the mighty whales that grace these waters. Humpback whales, known for their acrobatic displays and haunting songs, captivate the imagination as they breach and slap their tails against the water's surface. Their sheer size and graceful movements leave spectators in awe, reminding us of the vastness and wonder of the natural world.

Orcas, or killer whales, are another iconic species that call Alaska's coastal waters home. With their striking black and white markings and intelligent social structures, these apex predators command respect and fascination. Observing a pod of orcas as they navigate the currents, hunt for prey, and engage in playful behaviors is an experience that leaves a lasting impression.

Additionally, the migration of gray whales along Alaska's coast is a spectacle to behold. These majestic creatures undertake an epic journey from their breeding grounds in Mexico to the nutrient-rich feeding grounds of Alaska. Witnessing the gentle giants of the ocean as they breach and spout is a humbling reminder of the interconnectedness of marine ecosystems and the incredible resilience of these magnificent creatures.

Encountering wildlife in their natural habitat is a privilege that Alaska offers in abundance. The experience of observing these remarkable creatures up close and personal fosters a profound appreciation for their beauty, their role in the ecosystem, and the need to protect their habitats. It serves as a poignant reminder of our responsibility as stewards of the natural world.

In summary, an Alaska cruise is a gateway to a world of captivating wildlife encounters. From soaring eagles and comical puffins to playful sea lions, enchanting sea otters, and majestic whales, Alaska's wilderness is a haven for a diverse array of species. Observing these creatures in their natural habitat is a humbling and unforgettable experience that deepens our connection with the natural world and instills a sense of wonder and reverence for the delicate balance of life on our planet.

In summary, Alaska's allure lies in its vastness, natural beauty, and cultural richness. From the towering glaciers and snow-capped peaks to the mesmerizing fjords and diverse wildlife, every aspect of this land beckons adventurers and nature enthusiasts. Embarking on an Alaska cruise is a passport to extraordinary experiences and indelible memories. Prepare to immerse yourself in the splendor of Alaska's landscapes, delve into its fascinating history and native cultures, and witness the wonders of nature that make this destination truly remarkable. A journey through Alaska's waters is an invitation to embrace the last frontier and create lifelong memories in one of the world's most awe-inspiring destinations.

1.2 Why Choose an Alaska Cruise?

When it comes to exploring Alaska, there is perhaps no better way to experience its wonders than through an Alaska cruise. Offering a blend of comfort, convenience, and unparalleled access to some of the state's most remote and awe-inspiring destinations, an Alaska cruise presents a unique opportunity to immerse yourself in the natural splendors of this remarkable region.

There are numerous reasons why an Alaska cruise is the perfect choice for experiencing the wonders of this vast wilderness. Among them, the opportunity to witness Alaska's stunning coastline and glaciers from a unique perspective stands out as one of the most compelling aspects of such a journey.

Cruising through Alaska's icy waters provides an unparalleled vantage point, allowing you to witness the majesty of the coastline unfold before your eyes. From the comfort of your ship, you'll have front-row seats to a magnificent show of nature's grandeur. As you glide along, the striking vistas of rugged cliffs, serene fjords, and picturesque bays will capture your imagination and leave you in awe.

The highlight of an Alaska cruise is undoubtedly the chance to encounter the breathtaking glaciers that adorn the coastline. These frozen giants, shaped by millennia of compression and movement, are mesmerizing in their scale and beauty. From the deck of your ship, you'll witness the awe-inspiring sight of calving glaciers, where massive chunks of ice break off and crash into the sea with a thunderous roar. The spectacle is both humbling and thrilling, reminding you of the sheer power and constant change that define Alaska's glacial landscapes.

The towering icebergs that dot the waters add to the dramatic ambiance, creating a mesmerizing panorama of shimmering blue hues. These floating sculptures, sculpted by nature's hand, take on fascinating shapes and sizes, presenting a captivating display of elegance and fragility. Observing these icy behemoths as they drift silently through the water evokes a sense of serenity and appreciation for the delicate balance of our planet's ecosystems.

An Alaska cruise also offers a unique opportunity to witness marine wildlife thriving in their natural habitats. The nutrient-rich waters along Alaska's coastline attract a rich diversity of marine creatures, making it a prime location for wildlife encounters. From the deck of your ship, you may spot magnificent humpback whales breaching, their massive bodies leaping out of the water before gracefully plunging back beneath the surface. The sight of these gentle giants in their natural environment is a breathtaking reminder of the interconnectedness of all life and the beauty of the natural world.

In addition to whales, Alaska's coastal waters are home to a myriad of other marine species. Keep your eyes peeled for playful seals and sea lions lounging on rocky outcrops, their sleek bodies basking in the warm sunlight. Marvel at the acrobatic maneuvers of dolphins as they frolic alongside the ship, seemingly dancing in the bow waves. And if you're fortunate, you may catch a glimpse of elusive orcas, also known as killer whales, as they traverse the waters in tightly knit family pods.

The wildlife encounters continue as you explore Alaska's pristine shorelines during port stops and shore excursions. From bald eagles soaring overhead to curious sea otters frolicking in kelp forests, the variety of wildlife you'll encounter is astonishing. The experience of observing these animals in their natural habitats fosters a deep appreciation for their beauty, resilience, and the need to protect their fragile ecosystems.

Choosing an Alaska cruise provides a unique opportunity to witness the stunning coastline and glaciers of Alaska from a privileged perspective. The front-row seats to calving glaciers, towering icebergs, and captivating wildlife encounters create a journey of unforgettable moments. Immerse yourself in the natural splendors of Alaska, and let the breathtaking beauty of the region's coastline and glaciers leave an indelible mark on your heart and soul.

Another compelling reason to choose an Alaska cruise is the abundance of onboard amenities and activities that guarantee a comfortable and enjoyable journey. Cruise ships that navigate the Alaskan waters are renowned for their exceptional service, luxurious accommodations, and a wide array of entertainment options, ensuring that every moment of your voyage is filled with relaxation and excitement.

One of the highlights of an Alaska cruise is the opportunity to experience unparalleled luxury and comfort in your onboard accommodations. Cruise ships offer a range of stateroom options, from cozy cabins to spacious suites, all designed to provide a haven of relaxation after a day of exploration. Immerse yourself in plush bedding, indulge in the finest amenities, and wake up each morning to breathtaking views of the ocean or coastline. The attention to detail and impeccable service from the ship's staff ensure that your every need is met, creating an atmosphere of indulgence throughout your journey.

When it comes to dining, an Alaska cruise presents a world-class culinary experience. The onboard restaurants offer a diverse selection of cuisines prepared by talented chefs, catering to a range of tastes and dietary preferences. From gourmet dishes showcasing locally sourced seafood to international specialties and exquisite desserts, every meal is a gastronomic delight. Whether you choose to savor a formal dining experience or opt for a more casual setting, the onboard dining venues are designed to please even the most discerning palates.

In addition to the culinary delights, Alaska cruises provide a wealth of entertainment options that cater to a variety of interests. Enjoy live performances by talented musicians, singers, and dancers in the ship's theaters, or be captivated by awe-inspiring shows featuring world-class acrobats and illusionists. You can also unwind in stylish lounges and bars, where talented mixologists craft signature cocktails as you mingle with fellow travelers or enjoy a quiet moment overlooking the ocean.

To enrich your understanding and appreciation of Alaska's unique culture and natural wonders, cruise ships offer enrichment programs and educational activities. Engage in lectures and presentations by experts in fields such as marine biology, ecology, and native Alaskan culture. Learn about the fascinating history and geology of the region, gain insights into the behavior and habits of the wildlife you encounter, and deepen your understanding of the local communities and their traditions. These enriching experiences enhance your Alaska cruise, allowing you to forge a deeper connection with the destination and enriching your journey with knowledge and appreciation.

When it's time to unwind and rejuvenate, Alaska cruises offer a wealth of relaxation and wellness amenities. Indulge in soothing spa treatments, from massages to facials, that rejuvenate your body and mind. Relax in spacious lounges or by the pool, basking in the warm sun and taking in the breathtaking views. Stay active in the onboard fitness centers equipped with state-of-the-art equipment or participate in fitness classes and wellness programs led by experienced instructors. Whether you seek tranquility or invigorating activities, the onboard amenities cater to your personal preferences, ensuring a well-rounded and fulfilling cruise experience.

Furthermore, Alaska cruises often include exciting shore excursions that allow you to immerse yourself in the destination's natural beauty and cultural heritage. From thrilling wildlife encounters and scenic helicopter tours to hiking expeditions and visits to local communities, these excursions offer a deeper exploration of Alaska's wonders beyond the confines of the ship. Engage in thrilling adventures, witness captivating wildlife up close, and create lasting memories as you step ashore and embrace the unique experiences that Alaska has to offer.

An Alaska cruise not only provides an extraordinary journey through the region's breathtaking landscapes but also ensures a luxurious and entertaining onboard experience. Indulge in world-class accommodations, savor delectable cuisine, and enjoy a variety of entertainment options that cater to all tastes. Take advantage of enrichment programs and wellness amenities that enhance your understanding and well-being. With a range of amenities and activities tailored to create a memorable voyage, an Alaska cruise promises an unforgettable combination of comfort, adventure, and relaxation.

Furthermore, an Alaska cruise provides the convenience of a well-planned itinerary, carefully curated shore excursions, and knowledgeable guides. You'll have the chance to explore charming coastal towns, hike through pristine forests, go whale watching, and participate in thrilling outdoor adventures, all with the guidance and expertise of experienced professionals.

Lastly, cruising Alaska allows you to cover a significant amount of ground while unpacking only once. With each day bringing a new destination, you'll have the chance to experience a variety of Alaskan highlights, from the majestic Glacier Bay National Park to the historic town of Skagway.

In summary, choosing an Alaska cruise offers a unique and comprehensive way to discover the wonders of this vast wilderness. With stunning landscapes, abundant wildlife, and a wealth of cultural experiences awaiting you, an Alaska cruise promises an unforgettable adventure of a lifetime.

CHAPTER TWO

Planning Your Alaska Cruise

2.1 Selecting the Right Cruise Line and Ship

Choosing the right cruise line and ship is a crucial aspect of planning an Alaska cruise, as it can greatly impact the overall experience and satisfaction of your journey. With numerous options available, it's important to consider several factors to ensure you make the best choice. Let's delve deeper into these factors:

Reputation and Expertise:

When planning your Alaska adventure, one of the most important considerations is selecting a cruise line with a strong reputation and expertise in the region. Alaska's coastal waters present unique challenges, including ice, narrow channels, and unpredictable weather conditions. Therefore, it is crucial to choose a cruise line that has a proven track record of providing exceptional service and a high level of customer satisfaction.

To begin your research, explore different cruise lines that operate in Alaska and delve into their reputations. Look for companies that have established themselves as leaders in the industry and have been consistently praised for their quality of service. Reading reviews and testimonials from previous travelers can provide valuable insights into the experiences of others and help you gauge the cruise line's performance.

Pay attention to aspects such as the level of customer service, the professionalism of the staff, and the overall satisfaction of passengers. Look for feedback regarding the cruise line's ability to handle the unique challenges of Alaska's waters, such as navigating through ice-filled fjords and narrow passages. Positive reviews from past travelers who specifically mention the cruise line's expertise and competence in these conditions can be a good indicator of their suitability for your Alaska adventure.

Additionally, consider the experience and knowledge of the cruise line's staff. Alaska's coastal regions require skilled navigation and an understanding of the local environment. Seasoned captains and crew members who have extensive experience in these waters can contribute to a safer and more enjoyable journey. Look for cruise lines that emphasize their expertise in navigating Alaska's waterways and employ staff with a deep understanding of the region's unique challenges.

Reputable cruise lines often invest in comprehensive training programs for their crew members, ensuring they are well-prepared to handle the intricacies of an Alaskan cruise. Experienced naturalists and guides who can provide informative commentary and lead shore excursions further enhance the overall experience. Their expertise can enrich your understanding of Alaska's wildlife, flora, and cultural heritage, allowing for a more immersive and educational journey.

Furthermore, established cruise lines tend to have a solid network of local contacts and partnerships. They collaborate with reputable tour operators and local communities, fostering meaningful cultural exchanges and providing authentic experiences. These connections allow passengers to engage with the local culture, witness traditional performances, and gain insights into the traditions and history of the indigenous peoples of Alaska.

By selecting a cruise line with a strong reputation and expertise in Alaska, you can have confidence in the quality of service and the ability of the crew to navigate the challenging coastal waters. This can significantly contribute to the overall enjoyment and safety of your journey. It is worth noting that reputable cruise lines often prioritize the preservation of the pristine Alaskan environment and implement sustainable practices to minimize their ecological footprint.

Conducting thorough research and evaluating the reputation and expertise of cruise lines operating in Alaska is paramount to ensuring a successful and memorable adventure. Look for cruise lines with a proven track record of providing exceptional service, high customer satisfaction, and a focus on navigating Alaska's unique challenges. By choosing a cruise line that prioritizes safety, has experienced staff, and offers enriching experiences, you can embark on an Alaska cruise that exceeds your expectations and creates lifelong memories.

Ship Size and Amenities:

When choosing a cruise ship for your Alaska adventure, it's important to consider your preferences regarding ship size and onboard amenities. Each option offers unique advantages that can enhance your overall experience.

Smaller ships typically accommodate fewer passengers, creating a more intimate and personalized atmosphere. This can foster a sense of community among fellow travelers and allow for more meaningful interactions with the crew. With fewer passengers onboard, you'll have more opportunities to engage with the ship's staff, naturalists, and guides who can provide personalized attention and share their knowledge about Alaska's natural wonders.

One significant advantage of smaller ships is their ability to access narrower channels and fjords that larger vessels might not be able to navigate. Alaska's coastal waters are adorned with breathtaking scenery, including majestic glaciers, picturesque fjords, and remote coastal communities. Choosing a smaller ship allows for a closer encounter with these awe-inspiring sights. You'll have the opportunity to witness calving glaciers up close, sail through narrow passages surrounded by towering mountains, and visit remote ports that are off the beaten path. This intimate approach enables a more immersive experience, giving you a deeper connection with Alaska's natural beauty and cultural heritage.

Moreover, smaller ships often prioritize the natural environment by implementing sustainable practices. They strive to minimize their ecological impact, ensuring that the pristine Alaskan wilderness remains preserved for future generations. If environmental conservation is important to you, selecting a smaller ship that embraces sustainability initiatives can align with your values.

On the other hand, larger ships offer an extensive range of onboard amenities and facilities that cater to diverse interests and preferences. These floating resorts feature multiple restaurants, bars, and lounges, providing a wide array of culinary options and dining experiences. Whether you're seeking gourmet cuisine, casual dining, or international flavors, larger ships often have a variety of choices to satisfy your taste buds.

In terms of entertainment, larger ships shine with their extensive offerings. You'll find theaters showcasing Broadway-style shows, live music performances, comedy clubs, and movie theaters. Additionally, larger ships often provide a vibrant nightlife scene, featuring nightclubs, casinos, and various themed parties. If you enjoy a bustling and lively onboard atmosphere, larger ships provide an abundance of entertainment options to keep you engaged and entertained throughout your journey.

Furthermore, larger ships typically offer a wide range of wellness and recreational facilities. These may include fitness centers, swimming pools, spas, saunas, and sports courts. Whether you prefer working out, relaxing in a jacuzzi, or participating in organized sports activities, larger ships have the infrastructure to cater to your needs.

Another advantage of larger ships is the availability of a diverse selection of shore excursions and activities. They have the capacity to offer a variety of options, ranging from scenic helicopter rides and kayaking adventures to cultural tours and wildlife encounters. This allows you to customize your Alaska experience according to your interests and preferences, ensuring that you have a fulfilling and enriching time on land as well.

Ultimately, the choice between a smaller or larger ship depends on your personal preferences and what you value most in an Alaska cruise. If you prioritize an intimate and personalized experience, along with the ability to access remote and pristine locations, a smaller ship may be the ideal choice. On the other hand, if you seek a wider range of onboard amenities, entertainment options, and a bustling atmosphere, a larger ship may better suit your preferences.

Consider your priorities, the type of experience you desire, and the activities and amenities that resonate with you. By carefully evaluating these factors, you can select the ship size and onboard features that align with your vision of an extraordinary Alaska cruise. Remember, regardless of the ship size, the breathtaking beauty of Alaska and the unforgettable memories you create will be the highlights of your journey.

Itinerary Variety:

Alaska, known as the Last Frontier, is a land of awe-inspiring natural wonders, rich cultural heritage, and abundant wildlife. When planning your Alaska cruise, it's essential to review the itineraries offered by different cruise lines to ensure they align with your interests and desired experiences. Alaska's diverse landscapes and attractions can be explored through various cruise routes, each highlighting unique aspects of this remarkable destination.

One of the prominent features of many Alaska itineraries is glacier viewing. Glacier Bay, Hubbard Glacier, and Tracy

Arm Fjord are among the iconic destinations that cruise lines often include in their routes. These glaciers are truly breathtaking, displaying their grandeur through massive ice walls and dramatic calving events. Witnessing these phenomena firsthand is a humbling and unforgettable experience. The serene beauty of the glacial landscapes, the vibrant blue hues of the ice, and the echoes of cracking ice provide a captivating spectacle that showcases the power and beauty of nature.

Glacier Bay National Park and Preserve, a UNESCO World Heritage Site, is a crown jewel of Alaska's glaciers. A cruise through this pristine area offers unparalleled opportunities to witness numerous tidewater glaciers, including the famous Margerie Glacier. As you navigate through Glacier Bay, you'll be immersed in a landscape of icy fjords, snow-capped peaks, and abundant wildlife. Keep your eyes peeled for marine mammals such as humpback whales, orcas, sea lions, and harbor seals, as well as a variety of bird species soaring above the rugged coastline.

Hubbard Glacier, located in Yakutat Bay, is another magnificent sight on many Alaska cruise itineraries. Known for its immense size and dynamic nature, Hubbard Glacier stretches for over six miles and stands as one of the most active glaciers in the state. Marvel at the towering walls of ice and listen to the thunderous cracks and rumbles as icebergs calve into the sea. The sheer size and power of Hubbard Glacier create an awe-inspiring atmosphere that showcases the raw beauty of Alaska's natural landscapes.

Tracy Arm Fjord, nestled in the heart of the Tongass National Forest, is a narrow fjord that meanders through towering cliffs and snow-capped mountains. This picturesque destination offers a mesmerizing combination of cascading waterfalls, emerald-green waters, and jagged glaciers. Cruise ships navigate the narrow passages, providing an up-close encounter with nature's wonders. Keep your camera ready to capture stunning views of Sawyer Glacier and the surrounding landscapes as you sail through this breathtaking fjord.

While glacier viewing is a prominent feature of many Alaska cruises, it's important to note that different cruise lines may have their own unique itineraries that highlight specific aspects of the region. Some cruise lines may focus more on wildlife encounters, taking you to prime areas for spotting whales, bears, eagles, and other charismatic Alaskan fauna. These itineraries often include stops at places like the Inside Passage, Kenai Fjords National Park, or the Kodiak Archipelago, where you can immerse yourself in the abundant wildlife and pristine natural habitats of Alaska.

For nature enthusiasts and wildlife lovers, Alaska offers a treasure trove of opportunities to encounter a diverse array of marine and land wildlife. If you're particularly interested in immersing yourself in the natural wonders of Alaska, you'll find that certain cruise lines prioritize wildlife encounters, crafting itineraries that take you to areas known for their abundant wildlife populations.

The Inside Passage is a popular route for many cruise lines, offering a scenic and wildlife-rich journey through a network of sheltered waterways along the coast of Southeast Alaska. This region is teeming with marine life, and the nutrient-rich waters provide a thriving ecosystem that supports a variety of wildlife. Keep your eyes peeled for humpback whales breaching the surface, their majestic tails fluking as they dive into the depths. Witnessing these gentle giants in their natural habitat is a truly awe-inspiring experience.

The Inside Passage is also home to several other marine mammal species, including orcas, Dall's porpoises, sea lions, and harbor seals. You might spot these captivating creatures as they navigate the waters or rest on rocky outcrops. The air is often filled with the calls of seabirds such as bald eagles, puffins, and cormorants, adding to the vibrant tapestry of Alaska's wildlife.

Another notable destination for wildlife encounters is Kenai Fjords National Park, located on the southeastern coast of Alaska. This pristine wilderness boasts a stunning combination of glaciers, fjords, and lush forests, making it a haven for a wide range of wildlife. Cruising through the park's icy waters presents opportunities to witness the majesty of calving glaciers and observe sea otters and seals lounging on floating ice. Keep your binoculars ready to spot sea birds, such as tufted puffins and common murres, nesting on the cliffs, and scan the shoreline for bears foraging for salmon.

The Kodiak Archipelago, located in the Gulf of Alaska, is another hotspot for wildlife enthusiasts. It's renowned for being home to the Kodiak brown bear, one of the largest bear species in the world. These impressive creatures roam the remote and rugged landscapes of Kodiak Island, providing a unique opportunity to observe them in their natural habitat. A visit to this region may include guided excursions to bear viewing areas, where you can safely observe these magnificent animals from a respectful distance.

In addition to bears, the Kodiak Archipelago is frequented by other wildlife, such as sea otters, sea lions, and various bird species. You might spot bald eagles soaring overhead or witness playful sea otters floating on their backs, cracking open shellfish with their nimble paws. Exploring the diverse ecosystems of the Kodiak Archipelago can be an extraordinary adventure for wildlife enthusiasts and photographers alike.

When selecting a cruise line with a focus on wildlife encounters, consider the expertise of their onboard naturalists and guides. These knowledgeable professionals provide insightful commentary, host educational presentations, and lead shore excursions to enhance your understanding of Alaska's unique wildlife and ecosystems. Their expertise and passion for the natural world can enrich your journey, allowing you to gain a deeper appreciation for the intricate balance of Alaska's wildlife.

If cultural experiences are a priority for you, look for cruise lines that visit ports with indigenous communities, such as Sitka, Ketchikan, or Haines. These towns offer opportunities to learn about Native Alaskan traditions, visit totem pole parks, and witness traditional performances.

Consider your preferences and interests when selecting an itinerary, ensuring that it aligns with the specific experiences you seek in Alaska.

Onboard Programs and Activities:

When planning an Alaska cruise, it's important to delve into the onboard programs and activities offered by different cruise lines. While traditional entertainment options are always available, some cruise lines go the extra mile to provide specialized programs that enhance your Alaskan experience and cater to a variety of interests and hobbies. These additional offerings can greatly enrich your journey and provide opportunities for personal growth and exploration.

One aspect to consider is the availability of naturalist lectures and educational programs. Alaska is a region teeming with unique flora and fauna, and learning about its ecosystems, wildlife, and conservation efforts can deepen your appreciation for the environment. Some cruise lines employ onboard naturalists who are experts in Alaska's natural history and offer engaging lectures and presentations throughout the voyage. These knowledgeable individuals share their insights into the behaviors of marine mammals, the geological forces that shape the land, and the delicate balance of the region's ecosystems. Attending these lectures can provide valuable knowledge and enhance your understanding of the wonders you'll encounter during your cruise.

If you have a passion for photography, seek out cruise lines that offer photography workshops or dedicated photo tours. Alaska presents an abundance of stunning landscapes, wildlife encounters, and dramatic scenery that are a photographer's dream. By participating in photography workshops led by professional photographers, you can sharpen your skills, learn new techniques, and capture breathtaking images of Alaska's natural beauty. These workshops often include instruction on composition, lighting, wildlife photography, and post-processing, allowing you to capture the essence of the Last Frontier through your lens.

For those with an artistic inclination, cruise lines may provide art classes or workshops conducted by talented artists. These sessions allow you to explore your creativity while surrounded by the inspiring landscapes of Alaska. Whether it's painting, drawing, or other artistic endeavors, you can unleash your imagination and create unique pieces of art that reflect the beauty and spirit of the region. These classes often cater to all skill levels, so even if you're a novice, you can discover a new artistic passion and take home a meaningful souvenir from your Alaskan adventure.

Culinary enthusiasts can also find cruise lines that offer cooking demonstrations and classes focused on regional cuisine. Alaska's culinary scene is influenced by its abundant seafood, wild game, and native ingredients. Taking part in cooking demonstrations allows you to learn about traditional Alaskan recipes, cooking techniques, and the cultural significance of different dishes. From preparing fresh salmon to crafting delicious seafood chowders, you can immerse yourself in the flavors of Alaska and bring a taste of the region home with you.

In addition to onboard programs, some cruise lines offer specialized excursions led by experts in various fields. These excursions allow you to explore Alaska in more depth and engage with the environment and culture on a deeper level.

For example, you might have the opportunity to join a guided hike led by a naturalist, where you can discover hidden trails, observe wildlife in their natural habitat, and gain insights into the local flora and fauna. Alternatively, you may have the chance to participate in cultural exchanges with indigenous communities, where you can learn about their traditions, crafts, and ancestral knowledge. These specialized excursions provide unique experiences that go beyond the standard cruise offerings, allowing you to connect with Alaska on a more personal and meaningful level.

When selecting a cruise line, take the time to assess the onboard programs and activities offered and consider how they align with your interests and hobbies. Review the cruise line's website, brochures, and itineraries to get a comprehensive understanding of the additional offerings available. Consider the types of programs that resonate with you and envision how they can enhance your Alaska cruise experience.

By choosing a cruise line that caters to your specific interests, you can maximize your engagement and enjoyment during the voyage. Whether you're seeking educational opportunities, artistic inspiration, culinary adventures, or immersive excursions, the right cruise line can provide a well-rounded experience that aligns with your passions and allows you to create lifelong memories.

In conclusion, selecting the right cruise line and ship is crucial to ensure a fulfilling Alaska cruise experience. By researching the reputation and expertise of cruise lines, assessing the ship size and amenities, considering the variety of itineraries, and exploring the onboard programs and activities, you can make an informed decision that aligns with your preferences and interests. An Alaska cruise is not just about the destination; it's also about the journey and the experiences along the way. By carefully considering these factors and selecting a cruise line that offers activities that resonate with you, you can embark on an unforgettable adventure through the captivating landscapes, cultural treasures, and natural wonders of Alaska.

2.2 Best Time to Visit Alaska

Alaska's cruising season generally runs from May to September, with variations depending on the specific cruise line and itinerary. Understanding the best time to visit Alaska can enhance your experience. Consider the following:

Peak Season: June, July, and August are undeniably the peak months for Alaska cruises, and for good reason. These months bring longer daylight hours and generally more favorable weather conditions, creating an ideal environment for exploring the wonders of Alaska. The extended daylight provides ample opportunities to fully immerse yourself in the stunning landscapes, capturing every detail and maximizing your time outdoors. The milder temperatures of the summer months also make it more comfortable to engage in outdoor activities and fully enjoy the natural beauty that surrounds you.

One of the significant advantages of cruising during the peak season is the vast array of itineraries and shore excursions available. Alaska offers a diverse range of experiences, and during the peak months, cruise lines strive to provide an extensive selection to cater to various interests and preferences. Whether you're drawn to glacier viewing, wildlife encounters, cultural exploration, or outdoor adventures, there is a wide range of itineraries to choose from. You can embark on a voyage that takes you to iconic destinations such as Glacier Bay, Hubbard Glacier, or Tracy Arm Fjord, where you can witness the awe-inspiring beauty of calving glaciers, towering ice walls, and breathtaking landscapes.

In addition to the diverse itineraries, the peak season offers an abundance of shore excursions that allow you to delve deeper into Alaska's natural and cultural treasures. From guided hikes through pristine wilderness trails to kayaking among icebergs, from whale-watching expeditions to visits to native villages, the options are plentiful. These excursions provide opportunities to engage with the environment, learn about the local history and traditions, and create unforgettable memories. The peak season ensures that you have access to a wide range of activities and experiences that showcase the best of what Alaska has to offer.

However, it's important to be aware that the popularity of the peak season also means that Alaska's ports and attractions can be more crowded during these months. The larger number of cruise ships and tourists may result in queues and a higher level of activity at popular sites. While this does not diminish the beauty and allure of the destinations themselves, it's worth considering if you prefer a quieter and more serene experience. If you are willing to embrace the vibrant atmosphere and enjoy sharing the experience with fellow travelers, the peak season can provide an exciting and dynamic ambiance on board and on shore.

To make the most of the peak season while minimizing the impact of crowds, consider a few strategies. Firstly, plan and book your shore excursions in advance to secure your spot and ensure you can participate in your desired activities. This allows you to create a well-rounded itinerary that aligns with your interests and maximizes your time ashore. Additionally, explore lesser-known ports or less-visited areas within popular destinations to discover hidden gems and avoid some of the crowds. By venturing off the beaten path, you can still experience the beauty of Alaska while enjoying a more intimate and tranquil setting.

Lastly, embrace the stunning natural landscapes and the vastness of Alaska itself. Even during the peak season, there are ample opportunities to find solitude and tranquility by immersing yourself in the untouched wilderness that lies beyond the bustling ports. Take advantage of the extended daylight hours to explore the untouched corners of national parks, hike lesser-known trails, or simply enjoy the serenity of a quiet spot with breathtaking views. Alaska's grandeur is not limited to the well-traveled routes, and venturing off the typical tourist path can provide a deeper connection with nature and a sense of discovery.

In conclusion, June, July, and August are undeniably the peak months for Alaska cruises, offering longer daylight hours, milder weather, and a wide variety of itineraries and shore excursions. While it's true that these months can be more crowded, proper planning and a willingness to explore beyond the popular attractions can help you make the most of your Alaska cruise experience. By embracing the unique offerings of each destination, immersing yourself in the natural wonders, and seeking out quieter moments, you can have a truly remarkable journey through the pristine wilderness and breathtaking landscapes of Alaska.

Shoulder Season: May and September are considered the shoulder months for Alaska cruises, offering a distinct experience compared to the peak season. These months provide unique advantages and considerations for those seeking a more tranquil and off-peak Alaska adventure.

May, in particular, presents a captivating opportunity for wildlife enthusiasts. As winter fades away and nature awakens, May offers a chance to witness the abundance of wildlife as they emerge from hibernation and begin their seasonal activities. Bears, in particular, become more active during this time, as they venture out in search of food sources along the rivers and streams. Observing bears in their natural habitat, catching salmon or foraging for berries, is a thrilling and unforgettable experience. Additionally, May provides an opportunity to see other wildlife such as eagles, seals, sea lions, and a variety of bird species as they thrive in their natural habitats without the hustle and bustle of peak season crowds.

One of the significant advantages of cruising during the shoulder season is the reduced number of tourists. May offers a quieter and more serene atmosphere, allowing you to explore Alaska's natural wonders with fewer crowds and a sense of exclusivity. You can enjoy more intimate encounters with nature and have a more immersive experience, as popular sites and attractions are less crowded. This provides a unique opportunity to appreciate the tranquil beauty of Alaska's landscapes and wildlife without distractions.

While May brings the advantage of observing wildlife and avoiding crowds, it's important to be aware that weather conditions during this month can be more unpredictable. As Alaska transitions from winter to spring, you may encounter varying weather patterns, including rain showers, fog, and cooler temperatures. It's essential to come prepared with appropriate clothing layers and rain gear to ensure your comfort and enjoyment. The changing weather also adds an element of excitement and unpredictability to your journey, making every day a new adventure.

On the other hand, September offers a different charm as Alaska transitions into autumn. One of the highlights of cruising in September is the opportunity to witness the spectacular fall foliage. The landscapes of Alaska come alive with vibrant hues of red, orange, and gold as the leaves change color, creating a breathtaking sight against the backdrop of glaciers and mountains. This season provides a unique and picturesque experience for photographers and nature enthusiasts alike.

Another advantage of cruising in September is the potential for discounted fares and deals. As the cruising season draws to a close, cruise lines often offer incentives to attract travelers, including reduced prices, onboard credits, or special promotions. This can be an appealing aspect for those seeking a more budget-friendly option or looking to make the most of their travel budget. Taking advantage of these discounts allows you to experience Alaska's beauty and wonders while potentially saving some money.

Similar to May, September also experiences more unpredictable weather conditions. As Alaska transitions from summer to fall, you may encounter cooler temperatures, increased rain, and the possibility of early snowfall in certain regions. It's important to pack accordingly with layered clothing and waterproof gear to adapt to changing conditions. Despite the potential for inclement weather, September still offers a unique and captivating experience for those willing to embrace the seasonal transitions.

When considering a cruise during the shoulder months, it's crucial to maintain flexibility and have realistic expectations. While the weather may be more unpredictable, Alaska's natural beauty and wildlife sightings are still abundant and awe-inspiring. Embracing the quieter atmosphere, taking advantage of potential discounts, and being prepared for changing weather conditions will enable you to have a rewarding and memorable Alaska cruise experience.

May and September serve as the shoulder months for Alaska cruises, offering distinct advantages for those seeking a more intimate and off-peak experience. May provides opportunities to observe wildlife and enjoy fewer crowds, while September delights with fall foliage and potential discounts. However, it's essential to be prepared for the unpredictable weather that characterizes these months. By embracing the unique offerings of the shoulder season, you can embark on a remarkable journey through the natural wonders of Alaska, creating lasting memories and connecting with the pristine beauty of this remarkable destination.

Wildlife Viewing: If witnessing Alaska's majestic wildlife, particularly bears and whales, is high on your list of priorities, the mid-summer months of June and July are generally regarded as the ideal time for wildlife viewing. During this period, a remarkable natural phenomenon takes place—the annual salmon run.

The salmon run is a spectacular event that occurs when various species of salmon migrate from the ocean to their freshwater spawning grounds. These spawning salmon attract a plethora of wildlife, including bears, eagles, and seals, who eagerly await the abundant food source. As a result, the chances of encountering bears in their natural habitat are significantly increased during June and July.

Alaska's coastal areas, such as Katmai National Park and Admiralty Island, are renowned for their bear populations, and observing bears in their natural environment is an awe-inspiring experience. As the bears congregate along rivers and streams to feast on the spawning salmon, you can witness their hunting techniques, playful interactions, and the sheer power and grace with which they navigate the waterways. The mid-summer months provide the best opportunity to witness this extraordinary wildlife spectacle, where you can observe bears up close and gain a deeper appreciation for their role in Alaska's ecosystem.

In addition to bears, mid-summer is also an excellent time for whale watching in Alaska. The nutrient-rich waters attract a variety of whale species, including humpback whales, orcas (killer whales), and minke whales. These majestic creatures journey to Alaska's coastal waters to feed on the abundant marine life that thrives during the summer months. Witnessing these gentle giants breach the surface, spout water from their blowholes, and gracefully glide through the pristine waters is a breathtaking experience that showcases the true magnificence of Alaska's marine ecosystem.

To enhance your chances of whale sightings, consider selecting an itinerary that includes areas known for their whale populations, such as the Inside Passage or Glacier Bay. Many cruise lines employ expert naturalists and marine biologists who provide educational lectures and lead guided whale-watching excursions. These knowledgeable guides offer valuable insights into the behavior and conservation efforts surrounding these remarkable marine mammals, enriching your understanding and appreciation of Alaska's marine life.

It's important to note that while June and July offer the highest probability of encountering bears and whales, wildlife sightings are never guaranteed in the wild. Alaska's wildlife operates on its own schedule, and their presence can be influenced by various factors, including weather conditions and food availability. However, by cruising during mid-summer when the salmon run is in full swing, you significantly increase your chances of witnessing these incredible creatures in their natural habitats.

When planning your Alaska cruise during the mid-summer months, it's advisable to consult with your cruise line or travel agent to select itineraries and excursions that specifically focus on wildlife encounters. Opt for cruises that provide ample time in areas known for bear and whale activity, and consider booking shore excursions led by knowledgeable guides who can maximize your wildlife viewing opportunities.

Remember that wildlife encounters are a privilege and should be experienced with respect for the animals and their natural habitats. Follow the guidance of your guides and adhere to responsible wildlife viewing practices, maintaining a safe distance and minimizing any disturbance to the animals. This ensures the well-being and preservation of Alaska's incredible wildlife for generations to come.

If your priority is wildlife viewing, especially bears and whales, the mid-summer months of June and July are generally regarded as the optimal time for an Alaska cruise. The salmon run during this period attracts bears to the rivers and increases the likelihood of whale sightings. By selecting itineraries and excursions that focus on these experiences and following responsible wildlife viewing practices, you can immerse yourself in the natural wonders of Alaska and create cherished memories of encountering these magnificent creatures in their pristine habitats.

Northern Lights: For travelers captivated by the mesmerizing phenomenon of the Northern Lights, cruising in late August or September presents an excellent opportunity to witness these ethereal displays in the darkened Alaskan skies. As summer transitions into fall, the longer nights and clearer skies increase the chances of experiencing the awe-inspiring dance of the Aurora Borealis.

The Northern Lights, also known as the Aurora Borealis, are a natural light display caused by the interaction of charged particles from the sun with the Earth's atmosphere. This phenomenon creates vibrant colors and patterns that paint the night sky, ranging from shimmering greens to shimmering pinks, purples, and blues. Witnessing the Northern Lights is a magical and unforgettable experience that leaves travelers in awe of the natural wonders of our planet.

Late August and September offer favorable conditions for viewing the Northern Lights in Alaska. As the sun begins to set earlier and the nights become progressively longer, there are increased opportunities to witness the dancing lights of the auroras. The darkness of the night sky provides the perfect backdrop for the vivid colors to come alive, creating a breathtaking spectacle.

Alaska's remote and unspoiled landscapes make it an ideal destination for Northern Lights viewing. Away from the city lights and light pollution, the vast wilderness offers optimal conditions for observing the auroras. Cruising along Alaska's coastline allows you to access pristine locations that are ideal for stargazing and Northern Lights sightings. Onboard the ship, you can enjoy unobstructed views from open decks or designated observation areas, ensuring an uninterrupted and immersive experience.

When planning your cruise for Northern Lights viewing, it's essential to keep in mind that the appearance of the auroras is influenced by various factors. The intensity and frequency of the Northern Lights are dependent on solar activity, geomagnetic conditions, and weather conditions. While late

August and September generally provide favorable conditions for Northern Lights sightings in Alaska, it's important to note that the auroras are a natural phenomenon and cannot be guaranteed.

To maximize your chances of witnessing the Northern Lights, consider selecting a cruise itinerary that ventures into regions known for their Northern Lights visibility, such as the Inside Passage or regions close to the Arctic Circle. These areas offer darker skies, fewer obstructions, and increased opportunities for clear views of the auroras. Additionally, choose a cruise line that provides educational programs and onboard experts who can offer insights into the science behind the Northern Lights, enhancing your understanding and appreciation of this celestial phenomenon.

Remember that patience and flexibility are key when it comes to viewing the Northern Lights. The auroras can be unpredictable, and they may appear for a short time or persist for hours. Be prepared to stay up late into the night and remain vigilant, as the Northern Lights can make their appearance at any moment. It's advisable to dress warmly, as the nights in Alaska can be chilly, especially in late August and September.

While the Northern Lights are undoubtedly a highlight of an Alaska cruise, it's important to embrace the overall experience and immerse yourself in the region's natural beauty. Alaska offers a wealth of other attractions and activities, such as breathtaking landscapes, wildlife encounters, and cultural experiences. Take advantage of the cruise's itinerary to explore the stunning coastal scenery, visit charming coastal communities, and participate in excursions that showcase the unique wonders of Alaska's wilderness.

In conclusion, for those who have a fascination with the Northern Lights, cruising in late August or September offers an excellent opportunity to witness this celestial spectacle. With longer nights and clearer skies, the chances of experiencing the Northern Lights in Alaska are increased during this period. By selecting an itinerary that maximizes Northern Lights viewing opportunities and being prepared for the unpredictable nature of this phenomenon, you can embark on a cruise filled with awe and wonder as you witness the mesmerizing dance of the Aurora Borealis in the darkened Alaskan skies.

2.3 Choosing the Perfect Itinerary

Selecting the right itinerary is key to experiencing the highlights of Alaska that interest you the most. Consider the following when choosing your perfect Alaska cruise itinerary:

Glacier Viewing: When selecting an Alaska cruise itinerary, it's highly recommended to look for options that include iconic glacier destinations such as Glacier Bay, Hubbard Glacier, or Tracy Arm Fjord. These remarkable natural wonders showcase the awe-inspiring beauty of Alaska's glacial landscapes and offer unforgettable experiences for travelers.

Glacier Bay National Park, a UNESCO World Heritage Site, is a highlight of any Alaska cruise that ventures into its pristine waters. As the ship enters the bay, passengers are treated to a breathtaking panorama of towering snow-capped mountains, shimmering glaciers, and pristine wilderness. Glacier Bay is home to numerous tidewater glaciers, which means these massive rivers of ice flow all the way from their origins in the mountains to the ocean. Witnessing the thunderous crack and splash as chunks of ice calve off the face of a glacier and plunge into the water below is a truly awe-inspiring sight. The experience of being surrounded by the raw power and immense beauty of nature is unparalleled.

Hubbard Glacier, located in Yakutat Bay, is another must-see glacier on an Alaska cruise. It is the largest tidewater glacier in North America, spanning a width of about 6 miles at its terminal face. As the ship approaches, the immense size of Hubbard Glacier becomes apparent, with its towering walls of ice and vibrant blue hues. Observing the glacier's slow movement and listening to the echoes of ice breaking off into the water is a humbling experience that reminds us of the ever-changing nature of our planet.

Tracy Arm Fjord, located south of Juneau, is a narrow and picturesque fjord renowned for its dramatic landscapes and abundant wildlife. As the ship navigates through the fjord, passengers are treated to breathtaking views of towering granite cliffs, cascading waterfalls, and pristine forests. The highlight of Tracy Arm Fjord is the twin Sawyer Glaciers— Sawyer Glacier and South Sawyer Glacier. These magnificent tidewater glaciers captivate with their icy blue hues and the occasional sight of calving ice. The tranquil beauty of Tracy Arm Fjord and the serenity that surrounds it create a sense of awe and tranquility.

Experiencing these iconic glacier destinations on an Alaska cruise allows travelers to connect with the raw power and grandeur of nature. The sheer scale of these glaciers is humbling, and witnessing their majestic presence is a testament to the forces that have shaped Alaska's landscapes over millennia. Each glacier has its own unique character and charm, offering a different experience and perspective on the immense beauty of Alaska.

To enhance the experience of visiting these glaciers, many cruise lines provide onboard narration and expert commentary, offering valuable insights into the geological significance and natural history of these remarkable landmarks. Additionally, smaller expedition-style ships often have the advantage of accessing narrower channels and fjords, allowing for a more intimate and up-close encounter with the glaciers.

It's important to note that access to some of these glacier destinations is regulated to protect the fragile ecosystems and ensure a sustainable approach to tourism. Glacier Bay, for example, has a limited number of permits for cruise ships to enter the bay each day, ensuring that the area is not overcrowded and the pristine environment is preserved.

Including glacier destinations like Glacier Bay, Hubbard Glacier, or Tracy Arm Fjord in your Alaska cruise itinerary promises awe-inspiring views of calving glaciers and stunning landscapes. These iconic natural wonders offer a glimpse into the raw power and beauty of Alaska's glacial landscapes, providing a humbling and unforgettable experience. Whether witnessing the grandeur of Glacier Bay, the immensity of Hubbard Glacier, or the serenity of Tracy

Arm Fjord, each glacier destination offers a unique opportunity to connect with the captivating beauty of Alaska's icy realms.

Wildlife Encounters: For nature enthusiasts and wildlife lovers, Alaska offers an incredible array of opportunities to observe and interact with diverse marine and land wildlife. When selecting an Alaska cruise itinerary, it's highly recommended to consider options that visit areas known for their abundant wildlife, such as the Inside Passage, Kenai Fjords National Park, or the Kodiak Archipelago. These regions are renowned for their rich biodiversity and offer unparalleled experiences for wildlife enthusiasts.

The Inside Passage, a scenic coastal route that stretches from southeastern Alaska to British Columbia, is a haven for wildlife. The nutrient-rich waters of this area support a diverse ecosystem, attracting a variety of marine mammals, birds, and other wildlife. As the ship cruises through the protected waters, passengers have the opportunity to spot humpback whales breaching, orcas swimming gracefully, and sea lions basking on rocky shores. The passage is also home to numerous bird species, including bald eagles, puffins, and a variety of seabirds, providing ample opportunities for birdwatching enthusiasts.

Kenai Fjords National Park, located on the Kenai Peninsula, is another wildlife hotspot. This pristine wilderness boasts stunning glaciers, fjords, and rugged coastline, making it an ideal habitat for a wide range of wildlife. One of the park's main attractions is its population of marine mammals, including seals, sea lions, and sea otters. Additionally, visitors may have the chance to witness the majestic sight of humpback whales feeding and breaching in the park's waters. Kenai Fjords is also home to land-based wildlife such as black bears, moose, and mountain goats, which can be spotted while exploring the park's scenic trails and coastal areas.

The Kodiak Archipelago, located in the Gulf of Alaska, is renowned for its population of brown bears. This remote and rugged region offers opportunities for observing these impressive creatures in their natural habitat. Cruises that visit Kodiak Island provide the chance to see brown bears fishing for salmon in the rivers, foraging along the shorelines, or tending to their cubs. The archipelago is also home to a variety of bird species, including bald eagles, puffins, and auklets, making it a paradise for birdwatchers.

When planning an Alaska cruise itinerary focused on wildlife encounters, it's important to consider the expertise and knowledge of the onboard naturalists and guides. Many cruise lines employ knowledgeable experts who provide educational programs, lectures, and guided excursions specifically designed to enhance passengers' understanding of the local wildlife and ecosystems. These experts can offer valuable insights into the behavior, habitat, and conservation efforts related to the wildlife species encountered during the cruise.

To maximize wildlife viewing opportunities, some cruise lines offer specialized excursions and activities. These may include whale-watching tours, guided hikes in search of bears, or kayaking adventures in areas frequented by seals and sea otters. These excursions provide unique opportunities to get closer to wildlife, observe their natural behaviors, and create lasting memories.

It's important to approach wildlife encounters with respect and adhere to responsible viewing practices. Cruise lines and naturalists emphasize the importance of maintaining a safe distance from wildlife, ensuring minimal disturbance to their natural behaviors and habitats. By following guidelines and respecting the animals' space, passengers can have meaningful and ethical wildlife experiences while minimizing any negative impact.

Selecting an Alaska cruise itinerary that focuses on wildlife encounters allows travelers to connect with the incredible diversity and beauty of Alaska's marine and land wildlife. From the abundant marine life of the Inside Passage to the breathtaking vistas of Kenai Fjords National Park and the remarkable brown bear population of the Kodiak Archipelago, these regions provide unforgettable opportunities for wildlife observation. By choosing an itinerary that visits these wildlife-rich areas and considering the expertise of onboard naturalists, passengers can immerse themselves in the awe-inspiring world of Alaska's wildlife and create cherished memories of their encounters with these magnificent creatures.

Cultural Experiences:

To fully appreciate the cultural heritage of Alaska, it is highly recommended to choose an itinerary that includes ports with indigenous communities. These towns provide a unique opportunity to immerse yourself in Native Alaskan traditions, explore their rich history, and witness vibrant cultural performances. Sitka, Ketchikan, and Haines are among the notable ports that offer a glimpse into the indigenous culture of Alaska.

Sitka, located on Baranof Island, is a captivating destination that showcases the rich cultural heritage of the Tlingit people. As you step ashore, you'll be greeted by the iconic Sitka National Historical Park, a place of great significance in Tlingit history. The park features a remarkable collection of totem poles, some dating back centuries, which serve as storytellers and symbols of ancestral traditions. Take a guided tour through the park to learn about the Tlingit culture, their relationship with the land, and the stories depicted by the intricately carved totem poles.

In Sitka, you can also visit the Sheldon Jackson Museum, which houses an extensive collection of indigenous artifacts, including ceremonial masks, intricately woven baskets, and traditional clothing. The museum provides a deeper insight into the diverse cultures of Alaska's Native peoples, including the Tlingit, Haida, and Tsimshian.

Ketchikan, known as the "Gateway to the Inside Passage," is another port that offers a rich cultural experience. This vibrant town is home to the Tlingit, Haida, and Tsimshian communities, and their artistic expressions are beautifully showcased throughout the city. One of the highlights of Ketchikan is the Saxman Native Village, where you can witness master totem pole carvers at work and marvel at the intricate details of these towering art pieces. Take a stroll through the village to learn about the legends and stories that the totem poles represent.

Ketchikan is also famous for its lively arts scene. Visit the Totem Heritage Center to explore an extensive collection of restored totem poles and delve into the history and significance of this traditional art form. The center also offers workshops and demonstrations where you can try your hand at carving or learn traditional Native Alaskan crafts.

Haines, situated in the scenic Chilkat Valley, is another port that provides an authentic cultural experience. This small town is home to the Chilkat Tlingit people, and their rich traditions and customs are celebrated through various cultural events and performances. One of the highlights of Haines is the Alaska Indian Arts Center, where you can witness local artisans at work, creating intricate designs on traditional crafts such as Chilkat blankets, hand-carved masks, and silver jewelry. Engage in conversations with the artists and gain insight into their techniques and inspirations.

Haines is also known for the Chilkat Bald Eagle Preserve, a sanctuary for the majestic bald eagles. Take a scenic boat tour through the preserve, where you can observe these magnificent birds in their natural habitat while learning about their cultural significance to the Chilkat Tlingit people.

In addition to these specific ports, many Alaska cruises offer cultural enrichment programs onboard. These programs may include lectures, demonstrations, and performances by Native Alaskan artists, storytellers, and dancers. These experiences provide a deeper understanding of the indigenous cultures and traditions of Alaska, allowing you to connect with the rich history and heritage of the region.

When visiting indigenous communities and cultural sites, it's important to approach them with respect and a willingness to learn. Take the time to listen to the stories and traditions shared by community members, ask questions, and engage in conversations. By showing genuine interest and appreciation, you not only contribute to the preservation of these cultural traditions but also foster a meaningful exchange between cultures.

Selecting an Alaska cruise itinerary that includes ports with indigenous communities provides a unique opportunity to immerse yourself in the rich cultural heritage of the region. Sitka, Ketchikan, and Haines are just a few of the ports that offer a glimpse into the indigenous cultures of Alaska, with opportunities to explore totem pole parks, visit museums, witness traditional performances, and engage with local artisans. These experiences allow you to gain a deeper understanding of the traditions, history, and artistic expressions of Alaska's Native peoples, creating a truly enriching and memorable Alaska cruise experience.

Outdoor Activities: If you're an outdoor enthusiast seeking thrilling adventures and a closer connection with Alaska's awe-inspiring natural surroundings, there are numerous cruise itineraries that cater to your interests. These itineraries offer a range of exciting activities such as kayaking, hiking, fishing, and dog sledding, allowing you to immerse yourself in the rugged beauty of Alaska.

Kayaking is a popular activity for exploring Alaska's coastal waters and getting up close to its majestic glaciers. Many cruise lines offer guided kayaking excursions that provide a unique perspective on the region's breathtaking landscapes.

Paddle through serene fjords, navigate among icebergs, and witness the stunning blue hues of towering glaciers. As you glide through the calm waters, keep an eye out for marine wildlife such as seals, sea otters, and even whales, which occasionally make appearances near the kayaks.

For those who enjoy hiking and trekking, Alaska's vast wilderness presents countless opportunities for memorable adventures. Some itineraries include guided hikes led by knowledgeable naturalists who can provide insights into the local flora, fauna, and geological features. Strap on your hiking boots and venture into the pristine wilderness, surrounded by towering mountains, lush forests, and cascading waterfalls. Whether you're exploring the temperate rainforests of Southeast Alaska or traversing the tundra in Denali National Park, hiking in Alaska is a remarkable way to appreciate the region's natural wonders.

If you're a fishing enthusiast or simply want to experience the thrill of catching your own dinner, Alaska's abundant waters offer incredible fishing opportunities. Many cruise itineraries include fishing excursions where you can try your hand at reeling in salmon, halibut, or trout. Cast your line into pristine rivers, lakes, or the open ocean and feel the excitement as you battle against a feisty fish. Not only will you have the chance to catch a prized fish, but you'll also witness the untouched beauty of Alaska's aquatic environments.

Dog sledding is another exhilarating activity that allows you to experience a quintessential part of Alaska's history and culture. Several cruise itineraries offer excursions to dog sledding camps where you can learn about the traditions of dog mushing and even take a thrilling ride on a dog sled. Feel the adrenaline rush as the team of powerful and highly trained sled dogs pulls you across snow-covered landscapes, providing a glimpse into the age-old practice of transportation in Alaska's remote regions.

In addition to these specific activities, Alaska's diverse landscapes offer opportunities for wildlife spotting, birdwatching, and photography. Keep your camera ready as you cruise through the Inside Passage, where you may spot humpback whales breaching, sea lions basking on rocky shores, and bald eagles soaring overhead. Take a Zodiac boat tour to explore remote bays and coves, or embark on a wildlife safari in one of Alaska's national parks to observe bears, moose, caribou, and a variety of bird species in their natural habitats.

When selecting an Alaska cruise itinerary that focuses on outdoor adventures, it's important to consider your fitness level and personal interests. Some excursions may require moderate physical exertion, while others may cater to beginners or offer more relaxed experiences. It's also essential to follow safety guidelines and instructions provided by knowledgeable guides and instructors to ensure a safe and enjoyable experience.

By choosing an Alaska cruise itinerary that offers opportunities for outdoor adventures, you can create unforgettable memories and forge a deeper connection with the remarkable natural landscapes of this majestic region. Whether you're kayaking among glaciers, hiking through pristine wilderness, fishing in Alaska's abundant waters, or experiencing the thrill of dog sledding, these activities will leave you with a profound appreciation for the untamed beauty of Alaska..

2.4 Essential Travel Documents and Requirements

Before embarking on your Alaska cruise, it's essential to ensure that you have all the necessary travel documents and meet the requirements for entry into the United States. Taking the time to prepare in advance will help ensure a smooth and hassle-free journey. Consider the following important factors:

Passport

A valid passport is an absolute essential when planning an international trip, including an Alaska cruise. It serves as your primary identification document and proof of citizenship, allowing you to enter foreign countries and re-enter your home country. When it comes to traveling to Alaska, it's crucial to understand the passport requirements and ensure that your passport is valid for the duration of your trip.

First and foremost, it is important to check the validity of your passport well in advance of your planned departure date. Many countries, including the United States, require that your passport remains valid for at least six months beyond your intended stay. This requirement is imposed by both airlines and immigration authorities to ensure that travelers have a valid and up-to-date passport throughout their journey. It is important to note that if your passport expires within six months of your departure date, you may be denied boarding or entry into the country, causing significant disruptions to your travel plans.

To check the validity of your passport, take a look at the expiration date printed on the bio-data page. This is the page that contains your personal information, including your photograph and signature. If your passport is nearing expiration or falls short of the six-month validity requirement, it is advisable to renew it as soon as possible. Passport renewal can be done through the passport issuing authority of your home country. Be sure to check the renewal process and requirements, including any necessary documentation, fees, and processing times. Planning ahead and renewing your passport in a timely manner will help avoid any last-minute complications or stress.

In addition to passport validity, it's also important to ensure that your passport is in good condition. Any significant damage, such as water damage, torn pages, or illegible information, may render your passport invalid. It's always a good idea to keep your passport in a secure and protective cover to prevent any damage during your travels.

Furthermore, it is worth noting that some countries may have additional entry requirements, such as a visa, in addition to a valid passport. Before traveling to Alaska, it's essential to research and understand the specific entry requirements for your home country. This information can typically be found on the official website of the embassy or consulate of the country you plan to visit. It's important to allow sufficient time to gather the necessary documents and complete any required visa applications, if applicable.

A Valid passport is an absolute necessity for international travelers visiting Alaska. Checking the validity of your passport and ensuring that it remains valid for at least six months beyond your planned departure date is crucial to comply with entry requirements imposed by airlines and immigration authorities. By taking the time to check and renew your passport, if necessary, you can embark on your Alaska cruise with confidence, knowing that you have met the essential passport requirements and can fully enjoy your journey without any disruptions or complications.

Visa Requirements: Depending on your citizenship and the country you reside in, you may be required to obtain a visa before entering the United States for your Alaska cruise. Visa requirements can vary depending on factors such as your nationality, the purpose of your visit, and the duration of your stay. It is crucial to determine the visa requirements well in advance of your trip to ensure a smooth and hassle-free travel experience.

To gather accurate and up-to-date information about visa requirements, it is advisable to visit the official website of the U.S. Department of State. The Department of State provides comprehensive and reliable information regarding visa regulations, application procedures, and any specific requirements based on your citizenship. The website will guide you through the process and provide you with the necessary details to understand which visa category you fall under and the steps you need to take to apply.

Alternatively, you can also consult your local embassy or consulate of the United States. The embassy or consulate will have the most current information and can guide you through the visa application process. They will be able to answer any specific questions you may have and provide guidance tailored to your circumstances. It is advisable to contact the embassy or consulate well in advance of your trip to allow ample time for the application process, especially if you need to schedule an appointment or provide supporting documents.

Applying for a visa typically involves a process that may require certain supporting documents, fees, and, in some cases, an interview. The specific requirements can vary depending on the type of visa you are applying for, such as a tourist visa (B-2 visa) for a vacation or a business visa (B-1 visa) for attending conferences or meetings. It is important to carefully review the visa application instructions and gather all the necessary documents to support your application. These documents may include your passport, proof of financial stability, travel itinerary, and evidence of ties to your home country.

It's important to note that the visa application process can take time, so it is advisable to start the process well in advance of your planned travel dates. Delays in visa processing can occur, and it is always better to have your visa secured ahead of time to avoid any last-minute complications or stress. Planning ahead and allowing ample time for the visa application process will ensure that you have the necessary documentation in hand before your Alaska cruise.

It is essential to determine the visa requirements based on your citizenship and country of residence before embarking on your Alaska cruise. Visit the official website of the U.S.

Department of State or consult your local embassy or consulate to gather accurate and up-to-date information regarding visa regulations and application procedures. Start the visa application process well in advance to allow sufficient time for gathering supporting documents, paying fees, and attending any required interviews. By understanding and fulfilling the visa requirements, you can ensure a smooth and enjoyable travel experience as you embark on your Alaska cruise.

ESTA or Visa Waiver Program: If you are a citizen of a country eligible for the Visa Waiver Program (VWP), you may be required to apply for an Electronic System for Travel Authorization (ESTA) before your trip to the United States. The ESTA is an automated system that determines the eligibility of travelers to visit the U.S. under the VWP. It is an online application process that allows citizens of eligible countries to travel to the United States for tourism or business purposes for up to 90 days without the need for a traditional visa.

Applying for the ESTA is a straightforward process that can be completed online. It is essential to apply for the ESTA well in advance of your planned travel dates to ensure approval and avoid any last-minute complications. The U.S. Customs and Border Protection (CBP) recommends applying for the ESTA at least 72 hours before your departure, although it is advisable to apply as soon as your travel plans are confirmed.

To apply for the ESTA, you will need to provide personal information such as your full name, date of birth, passport details, contact information, and information about your travel plans. It is important to ensure that all the information provided is accurate and matches the details on your passport. Additionally, you may be required to answer a series of security-related questions as part of the application process.

Once you have submitted your ESTA application, it will be reviewed by the CBP. In most cases, the response is provided almost immediately, but it is possible that additional processing time may be required. It is advisable to check the status of your application periodically to ensure timely approval.

It's important to note that obtaining an approved ESTA does not guarantee entry into the United States. The final decision regarding your entry is made by the U.S. Customs and Border Protection officer when you arrive at the port of entry. It is essential to carry a printed copy of your approved ESTA with you when you travel as it may be requested by the airline and immigration authorities.

The ESTA is valid for a period of two years from the date of approval or until the expiration of your passport, whichever comes first. During this time, you can use the same ESTA for multiple trips to the United States, as long as each visit is within the 90-day limit. If your ESTA expires while you are in the United States, it does not affect your duration of stay, but you will need to obtain a new approved ESTA for any subsequent trips.

It is important to note that the ESTA is only applicable for travel under the Visa Waiver Program. If you plan to stay in the United States for more than 90 days or for purposes other than tourism or business, you will need to apply for an appropriate visa.

In conclusion, if you are a citizen of a country eligible for the Visa Waiver Program, applying for an Electronic System for Travel Authorization (ESTA) is an essential step before your trip to the United States. The ESTA allows for visa-free travel for up to 90 days for tourism or business purposes. Apply for the ESTA well in advance of your travel dates to ensure approval and to avoid any last-minute complications. Make sure to carry a printed copy of your approved ESTA with you when you travel. By following these steps, you can ensure a smooth and hassle-free entry into the United States for your Alaska cruise.

Vaccinations and Health Requirements: Before embarking on your Alaska cruise, it is crucial to prioritize your health and well-being by checking if any vaccinations or health requirements are recommended or mandatory for travelers. Ensuring that you are properly vaccinated and prepared can help prevent the spread of diseases and protect both yourself and the local communities you will encounter during your journey. The specific requirements may vary based on factors such as your home country, recent travel history, and personal health factors.

To obtain accurate and up-to-date information regarding vaccinations and health recommendations for travelers to Alaska, it is advisable to consult with your healthcare provider or visit the official website of the Centers for Disease Control and Prevention (CDC). The CDC provides comprehensive guidelines and recommendations for international travel, including specific guidance for different destinations and regions.

Your healthcare provider can assess your individual health history, current immunization status, and any specific health concerns you may have. They can provide personalized advice and recommendations tailored to your needs. They will consider factors such as your age, underlying health conditions, and the specific activities you plan to engage in during your Alaska cruise.

The CDC website is an invaluable resource that provides information on recommended vaccinations for international travelers. It offers guidance on routine vaccinations, as well as region-specific recommendations and any necessary travel-related vaccines. The website also provides important information on other health concerns and precautions, such as food and water safety, insect-borne diseases, and general health tips for travelers.

It's important to note that some vaccinations may require multiple doses or take time to become effective, so it is advisable to consult your healthcare provider well in advance of your travel dates. This will allow sufficient time to complete any necessary vaccinations and ensure that you are adequately protected before your journey.

Additionally, it is recommended to carry a copy of your vaccination records with you during your trip. This will serve as proof of your immunization status and can be helpful in case it is required for entry into certain countries or if you need medical attention while traveling.

In addition to vaccinations, it is also important to take general health precautions during your Alaska cruise. These include practicing good hygiene, such as regular handwashing, using hand sanitizers, and avoiding close contact with individuals who are sick. It is also advisable to be mindful of food and water safety, consuming only well-cooked or properly treated food and drinking bottled water or water that has been adequately purified.

Furthermore, it's a good idea to have travel insurance that covers medical expenses, as unforeseen health issues or accidents can occur during your journey. Travel insurance can provide financial protection and peace of mind in case of unexpected medical emergencies or the need for medical evacuation.

By being proactive and seeking the necessary health information and vaccinations, you can ensure a safe and healthy journey to Alaska. Remember to consult with your healthcare provider, stay informed through official sources like the CDC, and take necessary precautions to protect your health and enjoy a memorable and worry-free cruise experience.

Travel Insurance: While planning for your Alaska cruise, it is essential to consider obtaining travel insurance as part of your preparations. While it may not be a traditional travel document, travel insurance is a valuable investment that can provide essential coverage and peace of mind during your trip. An Alaska cruise, like any other travel experience, can be subject to unexpected events or circumstances, and having travel insurance can help protect you financially and provide assistance when you need it most.

One of the primary benefits of travel insurance is coverage for trip cancellation or interruption. Life is unpredictable, and unforeseen events such as illness, injury, or a family emergency can disrupt your travel plans. With travel insurance, you can be reimbursed for non-refundable expenses if you need to cancel your trip before departure or if you have to cut it short due to covered reasons. This can include expenses like cruise fares, airfare, accommodations, and pre-paid excursions.

Medical emergencies can also occur during your Alaska cruise, and the cost of healthcare services in a foreign country can be exorbitant. Travel insurance typically includes medical coverage that can help pay for necessary medical treatment, hospital stays, and emergency medical evacuations if needed. It is crucial to review the policy's coverage limits and ensure that it includes medical expenses incurred during cruises.

Another aspect to consider is coverage for lost or delayed luggage. It's not uncommon for luggage to get misplaced or delayed during air travel or transfers. With travel insurance, you can receive reimbursement for essential items you need to purchase while your luggage is being located or replaced. This coverage can help ease the inconvenience and ensure you have the necessary items during your cruise.

Travel insurance can also provide coverage for other potential travel-related issues such as trip delays, missed connections, or travel document loss. These situations can cause significant stress and financial burdens, but with the right insurance coverage, you can receive assistance and reimbursement for additional expenses incurred due to these events.

When selecting a travel insurance policy, it is essential to carefully review the coverage and terms to ensure it meets your specific needs. Consider factors such as the coverage limits, exclusions, deductibles, and any pre-existing conditions. Each policy may have different levels of coverage and optional add-ons, so it's important to understand what is included and what is not.

Additionally, it is advisable to compare different insurance providers and policies to find the one that offers the best value and coverage for your Alaska cruise. Read customer reviews and consider recommendations from trusted sources to assess the reputation and reliability of the insurance provider.

Before purchasing travel insurance, it's important to understand any existing coverage you may already have through other sources, such as credit cards or existing insurance policies. Some credit cards offer travel insurance as a benefit, and your existing health insurance or homeowner's insurance may provide certain coverage for travel-related incidents. However, it is essential to evaluate the extent of coverage and any limitations to determine if additional travel insurance is necessary to supplement your existing coverage.

In conclusion, obtaining travel insurance is highly recommended for any cruise, including an Alaska cruise. It provides essential coverage and protection against unforeseen circumstances that could disrupt your travel plans or result in unexpected expenses. By carefully reviewing the coverage, comparing different policies, and selecting the right insurance for your needs, you can have peace of mind and enjoy your Alaska cruise with confidence, knowing that you are protected financially in case of unexpected events.

It's crucial to complete all necessary travel document requirements well in advance of your Alaska cruise. Failure to comply with entry requirements could result in denied boarding or entry into the United States, potentially disrupting your travel plans. Stay organized, keep copies of important documents, and ensure that you have everything in order before setting sail on your Alaska adventure.

By taking the time to prepare and fulfill the required travel document and entry requirements, you can embark on your Alaska cruise with peace of mind, knowing that you have taken the necessary steps to ensure a smooth and enjoyable journey.

2.5 Packing Tips for an Alaska Cruise

Packing appropriately for an Alaska cruise ensures your comfort and enjoyment throughout your journey. Consider the following packing tips:

Layered Clothing: Alaska's weather is known for its unpredictability, ranging from mild and sunny to cold and rainy, even during the summer months. To ensure your comfort and preparedness for varying weather conditions, it is advisable to pack a versatile wardrobe with layers that can be easily added or removed as needed.

When packing for an Alaska cruise, consider including lightweight base layers as the foundation of your outfit. These base layers, such as moisture-wicking shirts and leggings, are designed to keep you dry and comfortable by wicking away sweat from your skin. They are ideal for regulating your body temperature, especially when engaging in outdoor activities or during periods of physical exertion.

Long-sleeve shirts made of breathable fabrics are also essential items to include in your suitcase. They provide an extra layer of warmth and protection against the elements while still allowing air circulation to keep you comfortable. Opt for lightweight materials like cotton or merino wool, which offer both insulation and breathability.

Sweaters or fleece jackets are great additions to your packing list. They provide warmth and can be easily layered over your base layers or worn alone, depending on the weather conditions. Look for sweaters or jackets that are lightweight and easy to pack, yet offer sufficient insulation.

A waterproof jacket is an absolute must when traveling to Alaska. The region is known for its rain and damp weather, so having a reliable and waterproof outer layer is essential. Look for jackets that are breathable and have sealed seams to keep you dry even during heavy rainfall. Additionally, consider a jacket with a hood for added protection against wind and rain.

Don't forget to pack a warm hat and gloves to protect your extremities from the cold temperatures. Choose hats that cover your ears and provide insulation, such as beanies or thermal hats. Opt for gloves that are waterproof or water-resistant to keep your hands dry in wet conditions. Additionally, consider gloves that offer touch screen compatibility, allowing you to use your electronic devices without having to remove your gloves.

It's also a good idea to pack comfortable and sturdy footwear suitable for outdoor activities and exploration. Consider waterproof hiking boots or sturdy sneakers with good traction to ensure stability and protection while walking on uneven terrain or wet surfaces.

Lastly, don't forget to pack essentials like sunscreen, sunglasses, and insect repellent. Even if the weather seems cloudy or cool, the sun's rays can still be strong, especially in high-altitude areas or near bodies of water. Protecting your skin and eyes from harmful UV rays is essential. Additionally, depending on the time of year and location, mosquitoes and other biting insects may be present, so having insect repellent can help make your outdoor experiences more enjoyable.

When packing for an Alaska cruise, it's important to be prepared for the unpredictable weather by including versatile layers that can be easily added or removed. Pack lightweight base layers, long-sleeve shirts, sweaters or fleece jackets, a waterproof jacket, a warm hat, and gloves. Don't forget to pack comfortable and sturdy footwear as well as essential items like sunscreen, sunglasses, and insect repellent. By packing thoughtfully and considering the varying weather conditions in Alaska, you can ensure your comfort and enjoyment throughout your cruise.

Comfortable Footwear: When preparing for an Alaska cruise, it's important to consider the footwear you'll need for both onshore excursions and onboard comfort. The rugged Alaskan terrain and potential wet conditions call for sturdy, waterproof shoes or boots that can handle uneven surfaces and provide traction.

For onshore excursions and exploring Alaska's breathtaking landscapes, it's crucial to have footwear that can withstand the elements and provide stability. Opt for hiking boots or shoes with good ankle support, durable materials, and a rugged outsole for enhanced grip. Waterproof or water-resistant features are highly recommended to keep your feet dry and comfortable, especially during rainy weather or when walking near bodies of water.

When selecting footwear for onboard comfort, consider packing warm socks and slip-on shoes. The ship's interiors are typically well-maintained and offer various amenities, so having comfortable slip-on shoes allows you to easily move around the ship without the hassle of laces or closures. Look for shoes with cushioning and breathable materials to keep your feet comfortable throughout your cruise experience.

In addition to sturdy shoes and slip-on options, it's also wise to pack a few pairs of warm socks. Alaska's climate can be chilly, even during the summer months, so having cozy socks will help keep your feet warm and insulated, especially during outdoor activities or when exploring colder regions.

Keep in mind that Alaska's weather can change quickly, and it's important to be prepared for different conditions. Consider packing additional items like waterproof shoe covers or extra pairs of socks to ensure your feet stay dry and comfortable in case of unexpected rain or wet conditions.

When packing your footwear, it's a good idea to utilize packing cubes or plastic bags to separate your shoes from other items in your luggage. This not only helps with organization but also prevents any dirt or moisture from transferring to your clothing.

Lastly, remember to wear your most comfortable and well-fitted shoes on the day of embarkation. This will ensure that you start your cruise with comfortable footwear and have the option to explore the ship and its amenities right away.

In summary, for an Alaska cruise, bring sturdy, waterproof shoes or boots suitable for walking on uneven terrain during shore excursions. Consider packing warm socks to keep your feet cozy. Additionally, slip-on shoes provide convenience and comfort onboard the ship. By having the right footwear for both onshore activities and onboard relaxation, you'll be prepared to fully enjoy your Alaska cruise experience.

Binoculars and Camera: When embarking on an Alaska cruise, one of the highlights is undoubtedly the opportunity to witness the incredible wildlife and scenic vistas that this majestic region has to offer. To fully appreciate and capture these unforgettable moments, it's essential to bring the right equipment, such as binoculars and a camera or smart phone with ample memory.

Binoculars are an invaluable tool for observing wildlife from the ship's deck or during shore excursions. Alaska is home to a diverse range of wildlife, including whales, bears, eagles, seals, and numerous bird species. With a pair of binoculars, you can get a closer look at these magnificent creatures, even when they are at a distance. Look for binoculars with a moderate magnification and a wide field of view to help you spot wildlife with ease and clarity. Compact and lightweight options are ideal for travel and can easily fit into your daypack or carry-on luggage.

Alongside binoculars, a camera or smartphone with ample memory is a must-have for capturing the breathtaking landscapes and wildlife encounters that Alaska has to offer. The natural beauty of Alaska is truly awe-inspiring, with towering glaciers, snow-capped mountains, pristine fjords, and vibrant wildflower meadows. To preserve these memories, make sure to bring a camera that suits your photography preferences. Whether you prefer a professional-grade DSLR camera or a compact point-and-shoot, ensure it has a sufficient memory card or additional storage options to accommodate the multitude of photos and videos you'll be capturing.

If you prefer using a smartphone for photography, today's smartphones offer impressive camera capabilities that can rival traditional cameras. However, it's essential to have enough storage space on your device or consider bringing external storage solutions to avoid running out of space during your trip. Additionally, carrying spare batteries or a portable charger is advisable to ensure you don't miss out on capturing those special moments due to a drained battery.

To enhance your photography experience and capture the best shots, familiarize yourself with the settings and features of your camera or smart phone before your trip. Experiment with different shooting modes, learn about composition techniques, and understand how to adjust settings for different lighting conditions. This knowledge will allow you to make the most of every photographic opportunity that presents itself.

Remember to respect wildlife and maintain a safe distance when observing and photographing animals. Follow guidelines provided by the cruise line, tour operators, or park rangers to ensure the well-being of both the wildlife and yourself. A telephoto lens or zoom feature on your camera can help you capture detailed images without disturbing the animals or compromising safety.

Lastly, protect your camera or smart phone from the elements by carrying a sturdy and waterproof camera bag or case. Alaska's weather can be unpredictable, and there may be instances of rain, splashes, or high humidity. Having a reliable protective case will safeguard your equipment and keep it in optimal working condition throughout your journey.

In conclusion, when embarking on an Alaska cruise, bring binoculars to spot wildlife from the ship and a camera or smart phone with ample memory to capture the breathtaking landscapes and wildlife encounters. With these essential tools, you'll be ready to immerse yourself in the awe-inspiring beauty of Alaska and create lasting memories of your extraordinary cruise adventure.

Essentials: When preparing for an Alaska cruise, it's important to pack a range of essentials that will enhance your comfort and convenience during the journey. Here are some items you should consider including in your packing list:

- Sunscreen: Even though Alaska is known for its cooler temperatures, the sun's rays can still be intense, especially during the summer months. Pack a broad-spectrum sunscreen with a high SPF to protect your skin from harmful UV rays. Don't forget to apply it generously on exposed areas, such as your face, neck, arms, and legs.
- Insect repellent: While Alaska is not typically plagued by mosquitoes or insects to the same extent as other destinations, it's still a good idea to bring a reliable insect repellent. This will come in handy during outdoor activities or excursions, particularly in forested areas or near bodies of water.
- Reusable water bottle: Staying hydrated is essential, especially during active shore excursions and hikes. Bringing a reusable water bottle allows you to refill it throughout the day, reducing waste and ensuring you have access to water whenever needed. Consider a bottle with insulation to keep your drinks cool during warmer weather.
- Backpack or day bag: A comfortable and sturdy backpack or day bag is essential for carrying your essentials during shore excursions and explorations.

Look for one with adjustable straps and multiple compartments to accommodate items like your camera, binoculars, extra clothing layers, snacks, and water bottle.
- Power adapter: Alaska, like the rest of the United States, uses Type A and Type B electrical outlets with a standard voltage of 120V. If you're traveling from a country with different plug types or voltage, make sure to bring a suitable power adapter to charge your electronic devices and keep them powered throughout the trip.

Necessary medications: If you take prescription medications or have any specific medical needs, ensure you have an ample supply of your medications for the duration of the cruise. It's also advisable to carry them in your carry-on bag rather than in checked luggage, to ensure they're easily accessible.

Formal Attire: When planning for your Alaska cruise, it's essential to consider the dining options and any formal or special events that may be offered on board. Many cruise ships have designated formal nights or themed events where guests can dress up and enjoy a more elegant dining experience. Here are some points to keep in mind when packing appropriate attire for these occasions:

- Check the cruise line's dress code policy: Different cruise lines have varying dress code policies, so it's important to review the guidelines provided by your specific cruise line. These guidelines will outline the suggested attire for formal nights or special events. Some cruise lines may have specific requirements, such as black-tie or formal dress, while others may have a more relaxed dress code.

- Pack cocktail dresses or evening gowns: For formal nights, consider bringing one or two cocktail dresses or evening gowns for women. Choose dresses that make you feel elegant and comfortable. Opt for classic styles and colors that can be easily accessorized. It's also a good idea to bring a shawl or light jacket to stay warm in air-conditioned areas of the ship.
- Consider suits or formal attire for men: Men can pack a suit or a tuxedo for formal nights, depending on the dress code specified by the cruise line. If a full suit or tuxedo is not required, a dress shirt, tie, and dress pants can create a more formal look. Bringing a blazer or sports jacket is also a versatile option for less formal events.
- Plan for themed events: Some cruise ships may organize themed nights or events during the cruise, such as a tropical night or a masquerade ball. If you're interested in participating in these events, pack appropriate attire according to the theme. This can include Hawaiian shirts, themed costumes, or masks, depending on the event.
- Be mindful of luggage restrictions: While it's important to pack appropriate attire, be mindful of the luggage restrictions set by the cruise line. Check the allowed number and size of bags, as well as any weight restrictions. If you have limited luggage space, consider versatile pieces that can be mixed and matched for different occasions.

- Rental options: If you prefer not to bring formal attire or if you have limited luggage space, some cruise lines offer rental services for formalwear. You can inquire about this option before your trip and arrange to rent formal attire on board the ship.

Remember, formal nights and special events are optional, and you can choose to participate or opt for more casual dining options if you prefer. It's always a good idea to bring a range of clothing options to accommodate different dining experiences and personal preferences. Additionally, check with the cruise line for any specific guidelines regarding dress code, as these may vary.

By packing appropriate attire for formal nights or special events, you can fully enjoy the elegant ambiance and create memorable experiences during your Alaska cruise.

CHAPTER THREE

Embarking on Your Alaskan Adventure

3.1 Port of Departure: Getting Started

Before embarking on your Alaska cruise adventure, it's important to familiarize yourself with the port of departure. This section will guide you through the essential aspects of getting started.

Choosing the Right Port Alaska cruises typically depart from ports such as Seattle, Vancouver, or Anchorage. Each port has its own advantages and logistical considerations that can help you make an informed decision about which one suits your needs and preferences best. Here's a closer look at each port:

Seattle:

Seattle is a popular departure port for Alaska cruises due to its convenient location and excellent transportation connections. Here are some advantages and logistics to consider:

- Accessibility: Seattle is well-connected with major airlines, making it easily accessible for travelers from various locations. It has a major international airport, allowing for convenient flights to and from the city.

- Pre-Cruise Activities: Seattle offers a vibrant city experience with iconic attractions such as the Space Needle, Pike Place Market, and the Museum of Pop Culture. Arriving a few days before your cruise allows you to explore the city and its cultural offerings.
- Port Facilities: The Port of Seattle offers modern and efficient facilities for cruise ship departures. It provides smooth embarkation processes, baggage handling services, and ample parking options for those arriving by car.

Vancouver:

Vancouver is another popular departure port for Alaska cruises, renowned for its stunning natural beauty and diverse cultural scene. Consider the following advantages and logistics:

- Scenic Setting: Vancouver is surrounded by picturesque mountains, lush forests, and the Pacific Ocean, providing a breathtaking backdrop for your cruise departure. The city itself boasts a vibrant downtown area with a variety of attractions, parks, and gardens.
- International Flights: Vancouver International Airport serves as a major transportation hub, offering a wide range of international flights. If you're traveling from outside North America, flying directly into Vancouver may be a convenient option.
- Port Facilities: The Port of Vancouver offers modern cruise facilities with efficient embarkation processes. The port is well-organized and easily accessible,

providing a smooth start to your Alaska cruise adventure.

Anchorage:

Anchorage, the largest city in Alaska, serves as a departure point for some Alaska cruises, particularly those exploring the Gulf of Alaska or cruises that combine land and sea journeys. Consider the following advantages and logistics:

- Land and Sea Combination: Choosing Anchorage as your departure port allows you to explore the breathtaking landscapes of Alaska's interior, including Denali National Park, before or after your cruise. It offers an opportunity to combine a land tour with your cruise experience.
- Scenic Train Journey: The Alaska Railroad operates between Anchorage and various interior destinations, providing a scenic and immersive way to reach or depart from the port. The train journey offers stunning views of Alaska's wilderness.
- Airport Access: Ted Stevens Anchorage International Airport connects Anchorage with major cities in the United States, making it accessible for both domestic and international travelers.

It's important to weigh the advantages, logistical considerations, and your personal preferences when choosing the port of departure for your Alaska cruise. Consider factors such as accessibility, pre-cruise activities, scenic surroundings, and any additional destinations or experiences you may wish to incorporate into your trip. By doing thorough research and evaluating your options, you can select the port that best aligns with your interests and enhances your overall Alaska cruise experience.

Transportation and Accommodation: Planning your journey to the port is an essential part of preparing for your Alaska cruise. Whether you're arriving by flight or opting for a road trip, it's important to consider logistics and find suitable accommodations near the port for a convenient and enjoyable stay before your cruise departure. Here's a closer look at each aspect:

Arriving by Flight:

If you're flying to the port city, consider the following tips to plan your journey:

Airport Selection: Research the airports in the vicinity of your chosen port. Determine which airport offers the most convenient connections and flight options for your departure. Consider factors such as flight availability, cost, and travel time.

- Transportation from the Airport: Explore the transportation options available from the airport to the port and nearby accommodations. This may include airport shuttles, taxis, ride-sharing services, or public transportation. Check if the port offers any shuttle services specifically for cruise passengers.
- Pre-Cruise Accommodations: Look for hotels or accommodations located near the port. Many hotels offer shuttle services to the cruise terminal, making it easier to reach your ship on the day of departure. Ensure that the hotel provides a comfortable and

convenient stay, considering factors such as amenities, proximity to attractions, and reviews from previous guests.

Opting for a Road Trip:

- If you're embarking on a road trip to the port, consider the following aspects:
- Route Planning: Determine the best driving route based on your starting location and the port city. Consider factors such as distance, driving conditions, and scenic routes. Plan for stops along the way to rest, refuel, and explore interesting attractions or natural wonders.
- Parking at the Port: Research the parking options available at the cruise port. Some ports offer onsite parking facilities, while others may have nearby parking lots or garages. Check the rates, availability, and security measures to ensure a smooth parking experience.
- Pre-Cruise Accommodations: Find accommodations near the port or along your road trip route. Look for hotels that offer parking facilities, especially if you plan to leave your vehicle parked during the duration of your cruise. Consider factors such as proximity to the port, amenities, and reviews.

Regardless of your mode of transportation, it's advisable to plan your journey in advance and make reservations for both transportation and accommodations. This helps ensure availability, especially during peak travel seasons. By planning ahead and finding suitable accommodations near the port, you can make the most of your pre-cruise stay, eliminate stress, and start your Alaska cruise adventure on a positive note.

Port Facilities: Getting acquainted with the amenities and services available at the port is essential for a smooth embarkation process and a hassle-free start to your Alaska cruise. Here's a closer look at the key aspects to consider:

Parking:

If you're arriving at the port by car, it's important to familiarize yourself with the parking options available. Research whether the port provides onsite parking facilities or if there are nearby parking lots or garages. Consider the following:

- Availability and Reservations: Check if parking spaces need to be reserved in advance, especially during peak travel seasons. Determine if there are any restrictions, such as vehicle size limitations or maximum parking durations.
- Rates and Payment: Review the parking rates and payment methods accepted at the port. Determine if payment is made in advance or upon departure. It's also a good idea to have cash or card available for payment.
- Security: Consider the security measures in place for the parking facilities. Look for well-lit areas, surveillance cameras, and security personnel to ensure the safety of your vehicle.

Baggage Handling:

Understanding the baggage handling process at the port will help ensure a smooth transition from your vehicle to the ship. Consider the following:

- Luggage Drop-Off: Find out where and how to drop off your luggage upon arrival at the port. Ports often have designated areas or personnel to assist with luggage drop-off, ensuring it reaches your stateroom onboard.
- Baggage Tags: Ensure that you have the necessary baggage tags provided by the cruise line. These tags typically include your stateroom number and other relevant information. Attach them securely to your luggage to facilitate proper handling and delivery.
- Carry-On Essentials: Pack a small carry-on bag with essential items such as travel documents, medications, valuables, and a change of clothes. This bag will stay with you throughout the embarkation process until your stateroom is ready.

Check-In Procedures:

Understanding the check-in procedures at the port will help streamline your embarkation process and minimize waiting times. Consider the following:

- Required Documents: Familiarize yourself with the documents you need to have on hand during check-in. This typically includes your cruise ticket, passport or other valid identification, and any additional documentation requested by the cruise line.

- Online Check-In: Many cruise lines offer online check-in options to expedite the process. Take advantage of this service to complete necessary paperwork, provide passenger information, and select preferences before arriving at the port.
- Security Screening: Prepare for security screening procedures similar to those at airports. Be aware of any restrictions on liquids or prohibited items and ensure that your carry-on bags are compliant.
- Boarding Time: Find out the designated boarding time specified by the cruise line. Arriving within the recommended timeframe will help avoid long queues and ensure a smoother embarkation process.

Understanding the layout of the port is also beneficial. Familiarize yourself with the terminal building, entrance points, and designated areas for parking, drop-off, and check-in. This knowledge will help you navigate the port efficiently and reduce any confusion or last-minute stress.

By getting acquainted with the port amenities, parking options, baggage handling procedures, and check-in processes, you'll be well-prepared to streamline your embarkation process and start your Alaska cruise with ease and peace of mind.

3.2 Life on Board: Ship Facilities and Amenities

Your Alaska cruise ship will be your floating home during the voyage. Understanding the ship's facilities and amenities will enhance your onboard experience.

Cabin Categories:

Exploring the various cabin options available on an Alaska cruise is an exciting part of planning your trip. From cozy interior rooms to luxurious suites with balconies, there are a range of accommodations to suit different preferences and budgets. Here's a closer look at the different cabin options and considerations to help you make the best choice:

Interior Rooms:

Interior rooms, also known as inside cabins, are typically the most affordable option. These cabins do not have windows or balconies but provide a comfortable and private space for resting and sleeping. Consider the following:

- Affordability: Interior rooms are often the most budget-friendly option, allowing you to allocate more of your budget to other aspects of your cruise experience.
- Darkness for Sleeping: The absence of windows can provide a darker sleeping environment, ideal for those who prefer complete darkness for restful sleep.
- Value for Money: If you plan to spend most of your time exploring the ship and participating in onboard activities, an interior room can be a cost-effective choice since you won't be utilizing a window or balcony as much.

Ocean View Rooms:

Ocean view rooms offer a window or porthole that allows natural light to enter the cabin and provides a view of the ocean or the surrounding scenery. Consider the following:

- Natural Light and Scenic Views: Ocean view cabins offer the advantage of natural light and the opportunity to enjoy views of the ocean or coastal landscapes from the comfort of your cabin.
- Mid-Range Option: Ocean view rooms typically fall within a mid-range price point, offering a balance between affordability and a view of the outside.
- Cabin Size: The size of ocean view rooms can vary, so be sure to check the square footage and layout to ensure it meets your comfort requirements.

Balcony Suites:

Balcony suites are the epitome of luxury and provide a private outdoor space to enjoy panoramic views of the ocean and the stunning Alaskan scenery. Consider the following:

- Private Outdoor Retreat: Balcony suites offer a personal balcony or veranda where you can relax, enjoy the fresh air, and take in the breathtaking views. It's a perfect spot for morning coffee or watching the sunset.
- Enhanced Space and Amenities: Balcony suites are generally more spacious than other cabin options, providing additional room for relaxation and often featuring upgraded amenities such as sitting areas, mini-fridges, and larger bathrooms.
- Premium Experience: Choosing a balcony suite elevates your cruise experience, offering a luxurious and indulgent setting to enjoy the beauty of Alaska's landscapes from the privacy of your own balcony.

When selecting a cabin, consider factors such as your budget, preferences for natural light and views, and the amount of time you plan to spend in the cabin versus exploring the ship or participating in activities. Additionally, pay attention to cabin layouts, bed configurations, and any specific features that may be important to you, such as accessible cabins or family-friendly options.

By exploring the different cabin options available and considering your preferences and budget, you can choose the perfect cabin for your Alaska cruise, ensuring a comfortable and enjoyable stay throughout your journey.

Dining Options: Discovering the dining options available on your Alaska cruise is an exciting part of planning your onboard experience. From formal restaurants to casual eateries and specialty dining venues, cruise ships offer a wide array of culinary choices to suit different tastes and preferences. Here's a closer look at what to expect and consider when it comes to dining on your cruise:

Formal Restaurants:

Most cruise ships feature one or more formal dining venues, often offering a diverse menu and an elegant dining experience. Consider the following:

- Reservation Policies: Formal restaurants may have reservation policies in place to manage dining times and ensure a smooth dining experience. Check if reservations are required or recommended, and familiarize yourself with the process for making reservations.

- Meal Timings: Formal restaurants typically offer set meal times for breakfast, lunch, and dinner. Take note of the designated dining times and plan your activities accordingly.
- Menu Variety: Formal restaurants often provide a range of menu options, including appetizers, entrees, and desserts, with choices to accommodate different dietary preferences. Look for a variety of cuisine styles and consider any special dietary needs you may have.

Casual Eateries:

In addition to formal dining venues, cruise ships typically offer casual eateries where you can enjoy a more relaxed dining experience. Consider the following:

- Buffet Restaurants: Buffet-style dining is a popular choice for casual meals on cruise ships. These venues offer a wide selection of dishes, allowing you to choose from various cuisines and customize your meals.
- Snack Bars and Cafés: Cruise ships often have snack bars and cafés where you can grab a quick bite or enjoy a light meal throughout the day. These options are perfect for casual dining on the go.
- Flexible Dining Hours: Unlike formal restaurants, casual eateries often have flexible dining hours, allowing you to enjoy a meal at your convenience during their operating hours.

Specialty Dining Experiences:

Specialty dining venues provide a unique culinary experience, offering a more intimate setting or showcasing specific cuisine styles. Consider the following:

- Reservations and Additional Charges: Specialty dining venues usually require reservations and may have an additional fee associated with them. Check the reservation process and any extra charges to plan accordingly.
- Unique Culinary Offerings: Specialty dining venues often feature themed menus or focus on a specific cuisine, such as steakhouse, seafood, or Italian. Explore the options available on your cruise ship and consider trying something different for a special dining experience.
- Exclusive Atmosphere: Specialty dining venues often offer a more intimate and upscale setting, providing a refined ambiance for a memorable dining occasion.

When planning your dining experiences, consider any dietary accommodations you may require, such as vegetarian, vegan, gluten-free, or allergy-friendly options. Cruise ships are typically equipped to handle a range of dietary needs, but it's a good idea to notify the cruise line in advance to ensure they can accommodate your specific requirements.

By familiarizing yourself with the ship's dining options, reservation policies, meal timings, and dietary accommodations, you can plan your onboard dining experiences accordingly. Whether you prefer formal dining, casual meals, or indulging in specialty venues, the variety of culinary choices on your Alaska cruise will enhance your overall cruise experience.

Entertainment and Activities: On an Alaska cruise, there is a plethora of onboard entertainment options and amenities available to enhance your overall experience. From live shows and musical performances to casinos and enrichment programs, as well as pools, spas, fitness centers, and sports facilities, there is something for everyone. Here's a closer look at what you can expect:

Onboard Entertainment:

Cruise ships offer a variety of entertainment options to keep you engaged and entertained throughout your journey. Consider the following:

Live Shows and Performances: Enjoy live performances by talented musicians, singers, dancers, and theater groups. From Broadway-style productions to comedy shows and acrobatic performances, there's a diverse range of entertainment to suit different tastes.

- Musical Performances: Many ships have live bands, solo musicians, or DJs performing in various venues onboard. Whether it's a soothing jazz ensemble, a lively party band, or a DJ spinning the latest hits, there's music to cater to different preferences and create a vibrant atmosphere.
- Casinos: If you enjoy gaming, cruise ships often feature onboard casinos where you can try your luck at a variety of games like slot machines, blackjack,

roulette, and poker. Note that age restrictions and responsible gambling policies may apply.
- Enrichment Programs: Some cruise lines offer enrichment programs that include educational lectures, workshops, and classes. These programs cover a range of topics such as history, wildlife, photography, cooking, arts and crafts, and more, allowing you to expand your knowledge while at sea.

Onboard Amenities:

Cruise ships are designed to offer a wide array of amenities for relaxation, wellness, and recreation. Consider the following:

- Pools and Water Features: Most cruise ships have pools and whirlpools where you can take a refreshing dip or lounge under the sun. Some ships even feature water parks or water slides for added fun, especially for families traveling with children.
- Spas and Wellness Centers: Indulge in spa treatments, massages, and beauty services at onboard spas. Relax in saunas or steam rooms, enjoy a rejuvenating facial, or book a full-body massage to unwind and pamper yourself.
- Fitness Centers: Stay active and maintain your fitness routine at the onboard gym and fitness centers. These facilities are equipped with a variety of exercise machines, free weights, and fitness classes led by professional instructors.
- Sports Facilities: Many ships feature sports facilities like basketball courts, tennis courts, mini-golf courses, and jogging tracks. Engage in friendly

competitions or enjoy a leisurely game while taking in the scenic views.
- Outdoor Spaces: Cruise ships often have expansive outdoor decks where you can soak up the sun, relax in loungers, or enjoy al fresco dining. These spaces provide a peaceful retreat with panoramic views of the surrounding landscapes.
- Kids and Teen Clubs: Family-friendly cruise ships offer dedicated areas and programs for children and teenagers. These clubs provide age-appropriate activities, games, and entertainment options, allowing younger travelers to socialize and have fun in a supervised environment.

As you plan your Alaska cruise, explore the onboard entertainment schedule to get a sense of the shows and performances available during your voyage. Additionally, check the ship's deck plans and amenities to familiarize yourself with the various facilities on offer. Keep in mind that specific amenities and entertainment options may vary depending on the cruise line and ship you choose.

By taking advantage of the onboard entertainment and amenities, you can enjoy a wide range of activities and experiences that cater to your interests, ensuring a memorable and fulfilling cruise vacation.

Shopping and Services:

On an Alaska cruise, you'll have access to a variety of onboard shopping opportunities and convenient ship services to enhance your experience. From duty-free stores and boutiques offering jewelry, clothing, and souvenirs to essential services like spas, salons, internet access, and laundry facilities, here's what you can expect:

Onboard Shopping:

Cruise ships often feature a selection of shops and boutiques, allowing you to indulge in some retail therapy during your voyage. Consider the following:

Duty-Free Stores: Take advantage of duty-free shopping, where you can find a wide range of products such as alcohol, tobacco, cosmetics, fragrances, and luxury goods. These stores often offer discounted prices compared to onshore retail outlets.

- Boutiques: Explore onboard boutiques that offer a curated selection of items, including clothing, accessories, jewelry, watches, and designer brands. You may find unique pieces and souvenirs to commemorate your Alaska cruise.
- Art Auctions: Some cruise ships host art auctions, showcasing a variety of artwork ranging from paintings and sculptures to prints and photographs. If you're an art enthusiast or looking to add to your collection, these auctions can be a great opportunity.

Ship Services:

Cruise ships provide a range of services to make your journey more comfortable and convenient. Consider the following:

- Spa and Salon: Treat yourself to a relaxing spa experience or pamper yourself at the onboard salon. Indulge in massages, facials, body treatments, hair

styling, manicures, pedicures, and other wellness and beauty services.
- Internet Access: Stay connected with onboard internet access. Many ships offer Wi-Fi packages that allow you to access the internet and stay in touch with family and friends or keep up with work if needed. However, note that internet access on ships can be limited and connection speeds may vary.
- Laundry Facilities: Cruise ships typically offer laundry services, including self-service laundromats or full-service laundry facilities. This is particularly convenient for longer voyages, allowing you to refresh your clothing and travel lighter.
- Photography Services: Capture the memories of your Alaska cruise with professional onboard photography services. Photographers are often available to capture your special moments during events, excursions, or formal nights. You can purchase prints or digital copies to take home as keepsakes.
- Guest Services: The ship's guest services desk is your go-to resource for any questions, assistance, or special requests you may have during your cruise. They can provide information, help with reservations, handle inquiries, and address any concerns you may have.

As you familiarize yourself with the ship's shopping opportunities and services, consider setting a budget for onboard shopping and pre-planning any spa treatments or salon appointments you may desire. Additionally, check the ship's daily schedule or newsletter for special events, promotions, or sales happening throughout your voyage.

By taking advantage of the onboard shopping opportunities and ship services, you can enjoy a well-rounded cruise experience that caters to both relaxation and convenience. Whether you're indulging in retail therapy, pampering yourself at the spa, staying connected with internet access, or making use of laundry facilities, these amenities and services add to the overall enjoyment of your Alaska cruise.

3.3 Safety Guidelines and Onboard Etiquette

Safety is a top priority on any cruise ship, and understanding the safety guidelines and onboard etiquette is crucial for a smooth and enjoyable journey.

Emergency Procedures Ensuring your safety and preparedness is of utmost importance when embarking on an Alaska cruise. Familiarizing yourself with the ship's emergency evacuation plans, muster station locations, and the procedures to follow during an emergency or evacuation drill is crucial. Here's what you should know:

Emergency Evacuation Plans:

Each cruise ship has comprehensive emergency evacuation plans in place to ensure the safety of all passengers and crew. These plans outline procedures for various emergency scenarios, such as fire, flooding, or other unforeseen events. Consider the following:

- Study the Information: Pay close attention to the emergency evacuation information provided in your stateroom or cabin. This typically includes a diagram

of the ship with evacuation routes and muster station locations.
- Read Safety Guidelines: Review the safety guidelines provided by the cruise line. These guidelines often cover important information on emergency procedures, life jacket usage, and evacuation protocols.
- Attend Safety Briefings: Participate in the mandatory safety briefings or drills conducted at the beginning of the cruise. These drills familiarize passengers with the emergency signals, muster station locations, and the actions to take in case of an emergency.

Muster Station Locations:

- Muster stations are designated areas where passengers gather during an emergency or evacuation. Familiarize yourself with the location of your assigned muster station. Consider the following:
- Listen to Announcements: Pay attention to onboard announcements that inform you about the location of your muster station and any changes to the designated area.
- Follow Crew Instructions: In case of an emergency, crew members will guide and direct passengers to their respective muster stations. Follow their instructions calmly and promptly.
- Take Note of Signs: Look for signage throughout the ship that indicates the direction to your muster station. These signs are typically displayed prominently on the walls or near stairwells.

Emergency and Evacuation Drills:

Cruise ships conduct mandatory emergency and evacuation drills to ensure that passengers are familiar with the procedures. Consider the following:

- Attend the Drill: Make it a priority to attend the emergency and evacuation drill conducted at the beginning of the cruise. This is an opportunity to learn about emergency procedures, locate your muster station, and understand the use of life jackets and other safety equipment.
- Listen and Observe: During the drill, pay attention to the crew members who provide instructions and demonstrate the proper use of life jackets. Take note of the emergency signals and the actions you need to take in case of an emergency.
- Ask Questions: If you have any doubts or concerns about the emergency procedures or evacuation plans, don't hesitate to ask the crew members present during the drill. They are there to ensure your safety and can provide clarifications or further guidance.

It is essential to remain calm and follow the instructions given by the ship's crew in case of an emergency. Remember to bring your life jacket to the muster station and do not use elevators during an evacuation unless instructed to do so.

By familiarizing yourself with the ship's emergency evacuation plans, muster station locations, and procedures, you will be better prepared to respond in the event of an emergency. Taking these precautions and participating in drills ensures your safety and the safety of fellow passengers during your Alaska cruise..

Health and Safety Protocols: Maintaining a safe and healthy environment is a top priority on any cruise ship, including those sailing to Alaska. To ensure the well-being of all passengers and crew, it's important to be aware of the ship's health and safety protocols. Here's what you should know:

Sanitation Practices:

Cruise ships have rigorous sanitation practices in place to prevent the spread of illnesses and maintain a clean environment. Consider the following:

- Enhanced Cleaning Procedures: Ships implement enhanced cleaning measures throughout the vessel, including common areas, dining venues, cabins, and high-touch surfaces. This helps minimize the risk of germ transmission.
- Sanitizing Stations: Look for hand sanitizing stations placed strategically around the ship. Use them frequently, particularly before dining, after using the restroom, or after touching surfaces in public areas.
- Cabin Cleaning: Cabin stewards regularly clean and sanitize your cabin, paying special attention to frequently touched surfaces like doorknobs, light switches, and remote controls.

Hand Hygiene:

Proper hand hygiene is crucial in preventing the spread of germs. Consider the following:

- Handwashing Facilities: Cabins and public areas are equipped with handwashing facilities, including sinks and soap dispensers. Take advantage of these facilities and wash your hands with soap and water for at least 20 seconds.
- Hand Sanitizer Availability: In addition to handwashing facilities, hand sanitizers are widely available throughout the ship. Carry a travel-sized hand sanitizer with you for convenience when soap and water are not readily accessible.

Illness Prevention and Outbreak Management:

Cruise lines have protocols in place to manage illness outbreaks and prevent the spread of contagious diseases. Consider the following:

- Health Declaration Forms: Before boarding, you may be required to fill out health declaration forms to ensure you are not experiencing any symptoms of illness. This helps to identify potential health risks and protect the well-being of all passengers.
- Medical Facilities: Cruise ships are equipped with medical facilities and trained medical staff to provide medical care if needed. Familiarize yourself with the location of the ship's medical center and its operating hours.
- Illness Reporting: If you experience symptoms of illness during the cruise, it's important to promptly report them to the ship's medical staff. This enables them to take appropriate measures to prevent the spread of illness.

- Isolation and Quarantine: In the event of an illness outbreak, the ship may have specific procedures in place for isolation and quarantine. Follow the instructions provided by the ship's crew and medical staff in such situations.

It's crucial to stay informed and comply with the ship's health and safety protocols throughout your Alaska cruise. These protocols are designed to protect the well-being of all passengers and create a safe and enjoyable environment onboard.

Additionally, familiarize yourself with any specific guidelines provided by the cruise line regarding illness prevention, outbreak management, or health-related requirements. This may include information on vaccination requirements, testing protocols, or any other measures put in place to ensure a safe cruising experience.

By adhering to the ship's health and safety protocols, practicing good hand hygiene, and staying informed about any specific guidelines, you contribute to the overall well-being of everyone onboard and help ensure a safe and healthy journey.

Onboard Etiquette: When cruising to Alaska, it's important to respect the ship's rules and regulations to ensure a pleasant and harmonious environment for all passengers and crew members. Here are some key areas to be mindful of:

Dress Codes:

Cruise ships often have specific dress codes for various occasions and venues. Familiarize yourself with the dress code guidelines provided by the cruise line. Consider the following:

- Formal Nights: Some cruises may have formal nights where passengers are encouraged to dress up in elegant attire. This typically includes cocktail dresses or gowns for women and suits or tuxedos for men. Follow the suggested dress code to maintain the desired ambiance.
- Casual Attire: During the day and in most dining venues, casual attire is generally acceptable. This includes comfortable and relaxed clothing such as shorts, t-shirts, sundresses, or resort wear.
- Specialty Restaurants: If you plan to dine at specialty restaurants, check if there are any specific dress code requirements. Some upscale dining venues may have stricter guidelines, requesting smart casual or semi-formal attire.

Smoking Policies:

Cruise ships have designated smoking areas and strict policies to ensure the comfort and safety of all passengers. Consider the following:

- Designated Smoking Areas: Smoking is typically restricted to designated outdoor areas on the ship. Familiarize yourself with the specific locations where smoking is allowed and respect these boundaries.

- Non-Smoking Areas: Be mindful of non-smoking areas, both indoors and outdoors. Respect the comfort of non-smokers by refraining from smoking in these designated areas.
- Electronic Cigarettes: Some cruise lines have policies regarding the use of electronic cigarettes. Familiarize yourself with the specific regulations to ensure compliance.

Noise Restrictions:

Maintaining a peaceful environment is essential on a cruise ship. Be considerate of fellow passengers by following noise restrictions. Consider the following:

- Cabin Etiquette: Keep noise levels low in your cabin, especially during nighttime hours when others may be resting. Avoid playing loud music, having loud conversations, or using electronic devices with loud volume.
- Public Areas: Be mindful of noise levels in public areas such as lounges, theaters, and hallways. Avoid shouting or engaging in disruptive behavior that may disturb others who are seeking a quiet environment.

General Etiquette:

Practice good manners and be considerate of others throughout your cruise. Consider the following:

- Queue Etiquette: Respect queues and wait your turn when boarding the ship, entering dining venues, or participating in activities. Avoid cutting in line, as this

can create frustration and inconvenience for fellow passengers.
- Politeness and Courtesy: Be courteous to fellow passengers and crew members by using polite language, saying "please" and "thank you," and showing respect in all interactions.
- Personal Space: Respect personal space and be mindful of others' comfort. Avoid intruding on others' personal space, and be aware of your surroundings to prevent accidental bumps or collisions.

By adhering to the ship's rules and regulations, practicing good manners, and being considerate of fellow passengers and crew members, you contribute to a positive and enjoyable atmosphere for everyone onboard. Remember that maintaining a respectful and harmonious environment enhances the overall cruise experience for all involved.

Responsible Behavior: When embarking on an Alaska cruise, it's crucial to understand the importance of responsible behavior, not only on the ship but also during shore excursions. Alaska's natural wonders are pristine and delicate, and it's essential to follow environmental guidelines, respect cultural sensitivities, and engage in wildlife conservation practices. Here's what you should keep in mind:

Environmental Guidelines:

Alaska is known for its breathtaking landscapes, rich biodiversity, and unique ecosystems. To help preserve the environment and minimize your impact, consider the following:

- Leave No Trace: When exploring nature, follow the principle of "Leave No Trace." Pack out what you pack in and dispose of waste properly. Avoid littering and respect the natural surroundings by leaving them undisturbed.
- Stay on Designated Paths: Stick to designated paths and trails when hiking or exploring natural areas. Straying off the path can damage fragile ecosystems and disrupt wildlife habitats.
- Respect Wildlife and Plant Life: Keep a safe distance from wildlife and refrain from feeding or touching them. Do not disturb nesting or breeding areas. Admire wildlife from a distance and use binoculars or zoom lenses for a closer view.

Cultural Sensitivities:

Alaska is home to diverse indigenous cultures, each with its own rich heritage and traditions. Show respect for local cultures and traditions by considering the following:

- Learn About Indigenous Cultures: Take the opportunity to learn about the indigenous cultures of Alaska. Respect their customs, traditions, and sacred sites. Seek permission before photographing or entering culturally significant areas.
- Engage in Cultural Experiences: Participate in cultural activities and events offered during shore excursions or onboard. Embrace the opportunity to learn and appreciate the traditions, music, dance, and art of the local communities.

- Purchase Authentic Local Products: Support local artisans and businesses by purchasing authentic local products and crafts. Ensure that the items you buy are ethically sourced and not made from protected or endangered species.

Wildlife Conservation Practices:

Alaska is renowned for its abundant wildlife, including bears, whales, seals, and numerous bird species. To protect these animals and their habitats, consider the following:

- Observe Wildlife Responsibly: When encountering wildlife, maintain a safe distance and avoid disturbing their natural behavior. Use binoculars or camera zoom lenses for a closer look. Do not approach or attempt to feed wild animals.
- Follow Whale Watching Guidelines: If participating in a whale watching excursion, follow the guidelines provided by the tour operator. Maintain a respectful distance from the whales and avoid surrounding them with boats.
- Minimize Noise and Light Pollution: During wildlife encounters, minimize noise and avoid excessive use of flash photography. Loud noises and bright lights can disrupt animals' natural behaviors and stress them.

By understanding the importance of responsible behavior, both on the ship and during shore excursions, you contribute to the preservation of Alaska's natural wonders and cultural heritage. Embrace the opportunity to learn, appreciate, and protect this remarkable destination for future generations to enjoy.

By familiarizing yourself with the port of departure, ship facilities, safety guidelines, and onboard etiquette, you'll be well-prepared to start your Alaska cruise adventure with confidence and peace of mind.

CHAPTER FOUR

Exploring Alaska's Coastal Towns

4.1 Juneau: Capital City and Gateway to Glaciers

Nestled in the heart of Alaska's Inside Passage, Juneau stands as a captivating destination that combines natural wonders and urban charm. As the capital city of Alaska, Juneau is a thriving hub of activity, offering a myriad of experiences for cruise travelers seeking adventure, culture, and breathtaking scenery. Serving as the gateway to numerous glaciers, Juneau entices visitors with its awe-inspiring landscapes and opportunities for exploration.

One of the most iconic attractions in Juneau is the magnificent Mendenhall Glacier. Located just a short distance from downtown Juneau, this colossal river of ice stretches over 12 miles, showcasing its grandeur and power. As you approach the glacier, you'll be mesmerized by its massive ice formations and the stunning blue hues that emanate from its depths. Witnessing the phenomenon of chunks of ice calving into the surrounding waters is an unforgettable experience, as the sound of the echoing cracks reverberates through the air. To fully appreciate the grandeur of Mendenhall Glacier, consider taking a guided tour or embarking on one of the hiking trails that wind their way through the enchanting surrounding landscapes. As you traverse the trails, you'll be rewarded with panoramic vistas, the chance to spot wildlife, and a closer connection to the natural wonders that define Juneau.

Beyond its glacier attractions, Juneau is also known for its vibrant cultural scene, which provides insight into the rich history and diverse heritage of Alaska. A visit to the Alaska State Museum is a must for those seeking a deeper understanding of the state's past. Through captivating exhibits, artifacts, and interactive displays, the museum tells the story of Alaska, from its indigenous cultures to the era of the gold rush. Delve into the traditions, art, and accomplishments of Alaska's Native peoples, and gain a newfound appreciation for their resilience and connection to the land. The museum also offers a glimpse into the turbulent times of the gold rush, where thousands of prospectors flocked to Alaska in search of fortune. Immerse yourself in the tales of the past, and gain an understanding of the challenges and triumphs that shaped the state's history.

For a taste of Juneau's wild frontier past, a visit to the famous Red Dog Saloon is a must. Stepping through its swinging doors and onto the sawdust-covered floors, you'll be transported back in time to the days of the gold rush. The saloon's rustic interior is adorned with historic memorabilia, giving it an authentic atmosphere that harks back to a bygone era. Enjoy live music performances as you sip on a cold beverage, and imagine the lively characters that once graced this iconic establishment. The Red Dog Saloon is a testament to Juneau's colorful past and serves as a reminder of the adventurous spirit that still permeates the city today.

As you explore Juneau, you'll also have the opportunity to partake in various outdoor activities that showcase the region's natural beauty. From hiking and kayaking to wildlife viewing and whale watching, there's no shortage of adventures to embark upon. Lace up your hiking boots and venture into the Tongass National Forest, the largest national forest in the United States. With its lush greenery, towering trees, and pristine waterways, the forest offers a tranquil retreat for nature enthusiasts. Traverse the trails that wind through the forest, marvel at the diverse flora and fauna, and breathe in the fresh, crisp air. Keep an eye out for wildlife encounters, as black bears, bald eagles, and Sitka black-tailed deer call this forest home.

For a truly unforgettable experience, consider taking a whale-watching excursion in the waters surrounding Juneau. These nutrient-rich waters attract an abundance of marine life, including humpback whales, orcas, sea lions, and porpoises. Board a comfortable vessel equipped with knowledgeable guides who will share insights about these magnificent creatures and their behaviors. As you cruise through the waters, keep your eyes peeled for the majestic breaches and graceful dives of the whales, creating memories that will last a lifetime.

In addition to its natural wonders, Juneau is also home to a thriving arts and crafts scene. Explore local galleries and boutiques that showcase the works of talented artists and artisans. From intricate Native Alaskan carvings to stunning jewelry inspired by the surrounding landscapes, these artistic creations offer a glimpse into the creativity and cultural richness of the region. Take the opportunity to support local artists and bring home a unique piece of Juneau as a memento of your journey.

Culinary enthusiasts will find a variety of dining options in Juneau, with a focus on fresh, locally sourced ingredients. Indulge in the flavors of Alaska with delectable seafood dishes, such as succulent king crab legs, pan-seared halibut, or wild salmon prepared in various ways. For a truly immersive experience, consider trying traditional Native Alaskan cuisine, which often incorporates local ingredients and showcases the unique culinary heritage of the region.

As the sun sets over Juneau, the city transforms into a picturesque landscape with a vibrant nightlife. Visit local bars and pubs to mingle with both locals and fellow travelers, sharing stories and experiences over a pint of craft beer or a cocktail inspired by the flavors of Alaska. Enjoy live music performances that showcase the talents of local musicians, creating an atmosphere of warmth and camaraderie.

Juneau's allure as a cruise destination lies not only in its natural beauty but also in the warmth and hospitality of its residents. The welcoming nature of the locals adds a special charm to the overall experience, making visitors feel at home in this remote corner of the world.

In conclusion, Juneau is a captivating destination that offers a unique blend of natural wonders, cultural richness, and urban charm. As the gateway to breathtaking glaciers, the city provides an opportunity to witness the raw power and beauty of nature up close. Immerse yourself in the grandeur of Mendenhall Glacier, explore the rich history at the Alaska State Museum, and step back in time at the iconic Red Dog

Saloon. Engage in outdoor adventures amidst the stunning landscapes, embark on whale-watching expeditions, and discover the vibrant arts and culinary scenes that make Juneau a truly unforgettable destination. Whether you're seeking adventure, cultural immersion, or simply a moment of tranquility surrounded by awe-inspiring landscapes, Juneau promises to deliver an experience that will leave a lasting impression on your Alaska cruise journey..

4.2 Skagway: Gold Rush History and Outdoor Adventures

Step back in time to the Gold Rush era as you set foot in Skagway, a charming town with a rich historical heritage. Known as the "Gateway to the Klondike," Skagway played a pivotal role during the late 19th century gold rush, attracting thousands of fortune seekers in search of their dreams of striking it rich.

As you explore Skagway, you'll feel as if you've stepped into a living museum. Stroll along the wooden boardwalks of Broadway Street, lined with colorful buildings that have been meticulously preserved from the gold rush era. These historic structures stand as a testament to the town's past, transporting visitors to a time when Skagway thrived as a bustling hub of activity. Admire the ornate facades and charming architecture, and imagine the sights and sounds that once filled these streets.

To delve deeper into Skagway's captivating history, make your way to the Klondike Gold Rush National Historical

Park. This park commemorates the gold rush era and offers a wealth of exhibits and interactive displays that bring the stories of the past to life. Join a guided tour led by knowledgeable rangers who will regale you with tales of the adventurous prospectors who braved the treacherous conditions in their quest for gold. Learn about the challenges they faced, the triumphs they celebrated, and the enduring spirit that defined this era.

Skagway's surrounding wilderness provides a playground for outdoor enthusiasts, offering a wide array of activities and adventures. Lace up your hiking boots and embark on a scenic trek along the historic Chilkoot Trail. This trail was once traversed by prospectors as they made their arduous journey to the Klondike goldfields. Follow in their footsteps as you hike through breathtaking landscapes, passing by crystal-clear lakes, dense forests, and rugged mountain peaks. Along the way, you'll gain a sense of the challenges and hardships faced by those who sought their fortunes in this untamed wilderness.

For a truly memorable experience, hop aboard the White Pass & Yukon Route Railroad. This narrow-gauge railway is a marvel of engineering and offers a thrilling ride through some of the most dramatic landscapes in Alaska. As the train chugs along, you'll be treated to panoramic views of towering mountains, cascading waterfalls, and pristine valleys. Marvel at the ingenuity of the railroad's construction, which allowed prospectors to access the goldfields with relative ease during the gold rush. The journey on the White Pass & Yukon Route Railroad is a testament to human determination and the indomitable spirit that defined the Klondike gold rush.

Skagway's allure extends beyond its historical and outdoor attractions. The town is home to a vibrant arts and culture scene, with local galleries showcasing the works of talented artists inspired by the surrounding landscapes. Explore the art studios and boutiques, and perhaps find a unique piece to take home as a cherished memento of your time in Skagway.

As you immerse yourself in Skagway's history, explore its outdoor wonders, and appreciate its artistic offerings, take a moment to savor the local cuisine. The town boasts a variety of dining options, from cozy cafes serving hearty comfort food to upscale restaurants highlighting the flavors of Alaska's bounty. Indulge in fresh seafood delicacies, such as succulent Alaskan king crab legs or pan-seared halibut caught from nearby waters. Immerse yourself in the vibrant dining scene, where the warmth and hospitality of Skagway's locals add an extra layer of charm to your culinary experience.

As the day draws to a close, Skagway's natural beauty takes on a magical quality. The surrounding mountains and forests provide a breathtaking backdrop as the sun paints the sky with hues of gold and pink. Capture the awe-inspiring momentson camera or simply pause to take in the beauty that surrounds you.

In the evening, Skagway offers a variety of entertainment options to round out your visit. Step into one of the local saloons, where you can enjoy live music performances that pay homage to the town's lively past. Listen to the melodies of folk, bluegrass, or country tunes, and let the music transport you to a bygone era. Engage in lively conversation with locals and fellow travelers, sharing stories and laughter as you unwind and soak in the vibrant atmosphere.

Skagway's charm extends beyond its borders, with the surrounding natural wonders inviting further exploration. Consider joining a guided tour or embarking on a boat excursion to explore the nearby fjords, where towering glaciers, cascading waterfalls, and abundant wildlife await. Keep your eyes peeled for seals, sea lions, and porpoises as they playfully navigate the icy waters, and be on the lookout for the majestic sight of whales breaching in the distance.

For those seeking a deeper connection to Skagway's gold rush history, consider participating in gold panning activities. Experience the thrill of searching for gold in the same rivers that drew fortune seekers over a century ago. Learn the techniques of gold panning from experienced guides, and perhaps uncover a glimmering nugget of history for yourself.

Skagway's enduring appeal lies not only in its captivating history and natural splendor but also in the warm hospitality of its residents. The town's friendly locals are always eager to share their knowledge and stories, ensuring that your visit is filled with memorable encounters and genuine connections.

Skagway is a captivating destination that immerses you in the excitement and allure of the Klondike gold rush era. From its meticulously preserved historic buildings to its scenic hiking trails and thrilling train rides, the town offers a wealth of experiences that transport you back in time. Explore the Klondike Gold Rush National Historical Park, soak in the natural beauty of the surrounding wilderness, and indulge in the local cuisine and arts scene. Whether you're a history enthusiast, an outdoor adventurer, or simply seeking a place of charm and character, Skagway is sure to leave a lasting impression on your Alaska cruise journey.

4.3 Ketchikan: Native American Heritage and Wilderness Excursions

Known as the "Salmon Capital of the World," Ketchikan is a vibrant coastal town nestled in the heart of Alaska's Inside Passage. Renowned for its rich Native American heritage and remarkable wilderness experiences, Ketchikan beckons travelers with its captivating blend of cultural immersion and natural beauty. Situated on Revillagigedo Island, Ketchikan is surrounded by lush forests, pristine waterways, and an abundance of wildlife, making it a paradise for outdoor enthusiasts and nature lovers.

Immerse yourself in the town's indigenous cultures at the Totem Heritage Center, a cultural treasure trove that showcases a remarkable collection of intricately carved totem poles. These towering wooden sculptures, adorned with intricate designs and symbols, are more than mere works of art—they are a testament to the traditions, stories, and beliefs of the Tlingit, Haida, and Tsimshian peoples. Stroll through the center and witness the artistry and storytelling behind each totem pole, gaining a deeper understanding of the rich cultural heritage that continues to thrive in Ketchikan.

To further explore Ketchikan's Native American heritage, consider joining a guided tour or cultural excursion that offers insights into the traditions and practices of the indigenous communities. Engage with knowledgeable guides who will share stories and legends, providing a glimpse into the spiritual connection between the Native peoples and the land. Participate in interactive experiences, such as traditional song and dance performances or hands-on workshops where you can learn traditional crafts like weaving or carving. These immersive encounters offer a profound appreciation for the vibrant living culture that shapes Ketchikan's identity.

For those seeking adventure, Ketchikan is a playground of outdoor activities and breathtaking landscapes. One of the most awe-inspiring destinations to explore is Misty Fjords National Monument, a remote and pristine wilderness accessible by boat or seaplane. Embark on a guided kayak tour through the calm waters of the fjords, surrounded by towering cliffs draped in verdant foliage and punctuated by cascading waterfalls. Paddle through narrow channels and hidden coves, marveling at the untouched beauty that unfolds at every turn. Keep an eye out for the diverse wildlife that calls this area home, including bald eagles soaring overhead, seals basking on rocky outcrops, and perhaps even black bears foraging along the shore.

Fishing enthusiasts will find themselves in paradise in Ketchikan, where the plentiful salmon runs attract anglers from around the world. Join a fishing excursion and experience the thrill of reeling in a prized catch, whether it be king salmon, coho salmon, or the elusive steelhead trout.

Expert guides will share their knowledge and techniques, ensuring an unforgettable fishing experience in the pristine waters surrounding Ketchikan. The reward for your efforts? Fresh Alaskan salmon—a true delicacy known for its rich flavor and succulent texture.

For a unique perspective of Ketchikan and its surrounding wilderness, consider taking a scenic floatplane tour. Board a small aircraft and take to the skies, witnessing the vastness and grandeur of the Alaskan landscape from above. Soar over majestic mountains, deep fjords, and emerald-green forests, capturing breathtaking aerial views that showcase the sheer magnitude and untouched beauty of this remote corner of the world. Your pilot will provide commentary, offering insights into the natural wonders below and sharing fascinating anecdotes about the area's history and geography.

In addition to its cultural and outdoor offerings, Ketchikan boasts a vibrant arts scene. The town is home to numerous art galleries and studios that showcase the works of local artists inspired by the surrounding landscapes and wildlife. From intricate Native American carvings and traditional basketry to contemporary paintings and sculptures, these artistic expressions capture the essence of Ketchikan's natural beauty and cultural richness. Take the time to explore the galleries and interact with the artists, gaining a deeper appreciation for their creative processes and the stories they convey through their art.

Ketchikan also offers a delightful culinary scene, with an emphasis on fresh seafood harvested from the surrounding waters. Indulge in a seafood feast at one of the town's waterfront restaurants, savoring the flavors of Alaskan king crab, halibut, or salmon prepared with culinary expertise. Experience the bounty of the sea, expertly crafted into delectable dishes that highlight the region's culinary heritage. Pair your meal with a locally brewed beer or a glass of wine, and enjoy the scenic views of the harbor as you dine.

Beyond the town itself, Ketchikan serves as a gateway to further exploration of Alaska's breathtaking wilderness. Consider extending your adventure by embarking on a multi-day expedition, such as a cruise or a wilderness tour, to remote areas such as the Inside Passage or Glacier Bay National Park. These journeys allow you to witness the raw beauty of Alaska's glaciers, fjords, and diverse wildlife up close, providing an unforgettable and transformative experience.

As your time in Ketchikan draws to a close, take a moment to reflect on the memories created in this remarkable coastal town. Whether it's the captivating stories shared by Native American elders, the exhilaration of kayaking through Misty Fjords, or the serenity of soaring above the vast Alaskan wilderness, Ketchikan leaves an indelible mark on your Alaska cruise adventure. Cherish the moments of cultural immersion, the connections made with locals, and the appreciation gained for the pristine natural landscapes that define this unique destination.

4.4 Sitka: Russian Influence and Stunning Wildlife

Situated on the picturesque Baranof Island, Sitka beckons with its unique blend of Russian heritage, stunning coastal landscapes, and abundant wildlife. As you step foot in this charming Alaskan city, you are immediately transported back in time, tracing the footsteps of the Russian settlers who once established their presence in the region. Sitka's history as the capital of Russian America is evident in its architecture, cultural influences, and preserved historical sites, offering a fascinating glimpse into the past.

Begin your exploration of Sitka by visiting its iconic landmarks, which serve as a testament to its Russian heritage. St. Michael's Cathedral, with its vibrant onion domes and ornate interior, stands as a magnificent example of Russian Orthodox architecture. Step inside this picturesque church, adorned with religious icons and intricate woodwork, and feel a sense of tranquility as you immerse yourself in its spiritual ambiance. Take a moment to admire the craftsmanship of the cathedral's design and reflect on the enduring legacy of the Russian settlers who built it.

Another must-visit site in Sitka is the Russian Bishop's House, a preserved historical landmark that provides a window into the lives of the Russian colonists who once called Sitka home. This beautifully restored house museum showcases the opulence and daily life of the Russian American Company's administrators. Explore the rooms adorned with period furniture, browse the exhibits that highlight the region's colonial past, and gain a deeper understanding of the significant role Sitka played during the era of Russian rule.

While Sitka's history is undeniably captivating, its natural beauty is equally mesmerizing. The city is blessed with a stunning coastal setting, surrounded by serene waterways, majestic mountains, and lush forests. Nature enthusiasts will find themselves in paradise as they explore the abundant wildlife that calls Sitka home. Look to the skies to witness the majestic flight of bald eagles, whose population thrives in the area. Observe playful sea otters as they frolic in the kelp forests, and keep your eyes peeled for the graceful breaching of humpback whales during their annual migration.

To fully immerse yourself in Sitka's natural wonders, consider taking a boat tour or excursion that allows you to get up close and personal with the marine life and rugged coastline. Cruise through Sitka Sound and admire the breathtaking vistas, with snow-capped peaks serving as a dramatic backdrop. Expert guides will provide informative commentary, enriching your experience with their knowledge of the local ecosystem and wildlife behavior. Capture memorable photographs of sea otters floating on their backs, eagles soaring overhead, and perhaps even the magnificent sight of a humpback whale gracefully breaching the surface.

For those seeking outdoor adventures, Sitka offers a wealth of opportunities to explore its pristine landscapes. Embark on a sea kayaking expedition, gliding through calm waters as you discover hidden coves, remote islands, and secluded beaches. Paddle along the coastline, marveling at the rugged cliffs and vibrant intertidal zones that teem with marine life. With each stroke of the paddle, feel a sense of serenity and connection with nature, as you navigate the same waters that the Russian explorers once traversed.

Another thrilling experience in Sitka is joining a guided bear-watching tour. These excursions take you to the remote corners of the region in search of Sitka's resident brown bears. Accompanied by experienced guides who possess a deep understanding of bear behavior and habitat, venture into the wilderness to witness these magnificent creatures in their natural habitat. Observe from a safe distance as the bears forage along the coastlines and rivers, gaining insights into their behaviors, feeding patterns, and social dynamics. This encounter with Alaska's apex predators is a truly awe-inspiring experience, providing a profound appreciation for the delicate balance of nature.

Beyond its historical and natural treasures, Sitka boasts a vibrant arts scene that reflects the region's cultural richness. Explore the local art galleries and studios, where you'll discover a diverse range of artistic expressions inspired by Sitka's natural beauty and cultural heritage. From traditional Native American carvings and intricate jewelry to contemporary paintings and sculptures, the artwork on display showcases the talents of local artists and their deep connection to the land. Take the time to engage with the artists, learn about their creative processes, and perhaps even acquire a unique piece of art as a memento of your visit.

Immerse yourself in Sitka's cultural events and festivals, which provide a deeper understanding of the community's traditions and celebrations. The Sitka Summer Music Festival brings world-class musicians to the city, filling the air with enchanting melodies that resonate throughout historic venues. Experience the magic of live performances as classical music weaves its way into the fabric of Sitka's cultural scene. The Sitka Fine Arts Camp, held annually during the summer, offers workshops and performances in various artistic disciplines, fostering creativity and artistic growth among both youth and adults.

As you explore Sitka's vibrant arts and cultural scene, take the opportunity to savor the flavors of the region. The city's dining scene showcases an array of culinary delights, with an emphasis on locally sourced ingredients and fresh seafood. Indulge in a feast of Alaskan king crab, halibut, or salmon, prepared with culinary expertise and accompanied by delectable side dishes that highlight the flavors of the region. Whether you choose a waterfront restaurant with panoramic views of the harbor or a cozy cafe tucked away in Sitka's charming streets, the culinary offerings will tantalize your taste buds and leave you craving for more.

Sitka's allure extends beyond the boundaries of the city itself, as it serves as a gateway to further exploration of Alaska's breathtaking wilderness. Consider extending your journey by embarking on a multi-day expedition, such as a cruise or a wilderness tour, to renowned destinations like Glacier Bay National Park or Admiralty Island. These extraordinary experiences offer an unparalleled opportunity to witness the raw beauty of Alaska's glaciers, fjords, and pristine landscapes, all while encountering a diverse range of wildlife in their natural habitats. Immerse yourself in the grandeur of towering ice formations, listen to the thunderous roars of calving glaciers, and marvel at the abundance of marine and terrestrial life that thrives in these protected areas.

As your time in Sitka comes to a close, you'll find yourself enriched by the captivating blend of Russian influences, stunning wildlife encounters, and breathtaking landscapes. Reflect on the moments spent exploring historical sites that bear witness to the city's rich heritage. Cherish the memories of encounters with wildlife, from eagles soaring overhead to whales gracefully breaching the surface. And remember the warmth of Sitka's artistic community, where creativity flourishes amidst the awe-inspiring natural surroundings.

Sitka's allure lies not only in its tangible treasures but also in the intangible sense of wonder and connection that it evokes. As you bid farewell to this remarkable destination, carry with you the spirit of Sitka—a place where history, nature, and culture intertwine to create an unforgettable experience.

CHAPTER FIVE

Cruising Alaska's Magnificent Glaciers

5.1 Glacier Bay National Park: A Natural Wonder

Glacier Bay National Park: A Pristine Wilderness of Ice, Mountains, and Wildlife

Glacier Bay National Park, located in southeastern Alaska, is a true natural wonder and a highlight of any Alaska cruise itinerary. This vast and pristine wilderness encompasses a mesmerizing landscape of glaciers, towering mountains, and a diverse array of wildlife. As you sail through the icy waters of Glacier Bay, be prepared to witness the awe-inspiring sight of massive tidewater glaciers calving into the sea, creating a spectacle that showcases the dynamic forces of nature.

Spanning over 3.3 million acres, Glacier Bay National Park is one of the largest protected areas for glacier ecosystems in the world. Its dramatic landscapes are a result of the relentless movement of ice over thousands of years. The park is home to more than 1,000 glaciers, each unique in size and shape, carving their way through the rugged terrain. These glaciers, including the famous Margerie Glacier and Grand Pacific Glacier, are the main attractions that draw visitors from around the globe.

As you venture into Glacier Bay, you'll find yourself surrounded by a pristine environment that seems untouched by human hands. The air is crisp, and the silence is broken only by the occasional sound of ice cracking or the distant call of a seabird. The waters of Glacier Bay are a tapestry of icy blues, reflecting the stunning glaciers and snow-capped peaks that line the horizon.

One of the most captivating experiences in Glacier Bay National Park is witnessing the phenomenon of calving. Tidewater glaciers, such as the Margerie Glacier, extend all the way to the water's edge. As the glaciers slowly advance, massive chunks of ice break off, or calve, into the sea with thunderous roars. These calving events create a powerful display, as icebergs of varying sizes plunge into the water, creating ripples that reverberate throughout the bay.

Glacier Bay is not just a land of ice and mountains; it is also a haven for wildlife enthusiasts. The park is teeming with a rich variety of animal species that have adapted to survive in this unique and challenging environment. One of the most iconic sights in Glacier Bay is the breaching of humpback whales. These majestic creatures migrate to the nutrient-rich waters of Alaska each year to feed, and their acrobatic displays are a sight to behold. As you cruise through the bay, keep your eyes peeled for the telltale signs of whales surfacing and their massive bodies leaping out of the water.

Sea otters are another charismatic species that call Glacier Bay home. These playful creatures can often be spotted floating on their backs, using rocks as tools to crack open their favorite food, shellfish. Watching them groom their fur or engage in social behaviors is a delightful sight.

Glacier Bay is also a haven for bird enthusiasts, with numerous species of seabirds soaring through the skies and nesting along the cliffs. The park is a prime habitat for bald eagles, and it's not uncommon to see these majestic birds perched on tree branches or soaring high above the fjords, their sharp eyes scanning the waters for fish.

On the rocky shorelines and sandy beaches, grizzly bears can often be spotted foraging for food. These magnificent creatures, with their powerful presence and lumbering gait, are a symbol of the untamed wilderness that surrounds Glacier Bay. Observing them from a safe distance is an unforgettable experience that highlights the raw beauty and natural balance of this ecosystem.

To explore Glacier Bay National Park more intimately, many cruise ships offer guided excursions on smaller boats or kayaks, allowing you to get closer to the glaciers and experience the serenity of this remote wilderness. These smaller vessels provide the opportunity to navigate through narrow channels and coves that larger ships cannot access, bringing you closer to the heart of the park's natural wonders. These excursions often include knowledgeable park rangers who serve as guides, sharing their expertise on the park's geology, flora, and fauna.

As you embark on a guided excursion, you'll find yourself in the midst of a majestic ice kingdom. The towering walls of ice, sculpted by centuries of glacial activity, surround you in a serene and ethereal atmosphere. The proximity to the glaciers allows you to witness their intricate details up close – the deep blue crevasses, the jagged peaks, and the constant movement as they continue to shape the landscape.

While cruising through Glacier Bay in a smaller vessel, you'll have the chance to witness firsthand the incredible power and beauty of calving glaciers. As you watch chunks of ice break free and crash into the water, you'll be captivated by the thunderous sounds and the resulting waves that ripple across the bay. The experience is humbling, reminding you of the dynamic nature of this ever-changing environment.

Throughout the excursion, the park rangers provide valuable insights into the geological processes that have shaped Glacier Bay. They explain how the glaciers have carved out deep fjords and valleys, leaving behind a mosaic of islands and channels that create a labyrinth for exploration. You'll gain a deeper appreciation for the delicate balance between ice and water, and the critical role that glaciers play in shaping the landscape and sustaining the surrounding ecosystems.

In addition to the glaciers, the park rangers share their knowledge about the rich biodiversity that thrives in Glacier Bay. They point out the various plant species that have adapted to survive in this harsh environment, such as the hardy alpine flowers and the resilient mosses that cling to rocks. They also provide insights into the interconnected web of life that exists within the park, from the smallest organisms to the largest predators.

As you navigate through the pristine waters, you may encounter seals basking on floating icebergs or swimming gracefully alongside your vessel. These marine mammals are well-adapted to the cold waters of Alaska and are often seen lounging and sunning themselves, occasionally curiously peering at passing visitors. The rangers share stories and facts about the different seal species that call Glacier Bay home, including the harbor seals and the less common but equally fascinating Steller sea lions.

Glacier Bay is a haven for bird enthusiasts, and the rangers help you identify the various seabirds that inhabit the park. From the elegant black-legged kittiwakes to the graceful glaucous-winged gulls, these birds are perfectly adapted to their coastal habitat. The rangers point out nesting sites, explain their migratory patterns, and share interesting facts about their behaviors and conservation efforts.

Throughout the excursion, the rangers also emphasize the importance of responsible and sustainable tourism in Glacier Bay. They highlight the measures taken to preserve this delicate ecosystem and encourage visitors to minimize their impact on the environment. By providing education and raising awareness, they hope to foster a sense of stewardship among visitors, ensuring that future generations can also experience the wonders of Glacier Bay.

As the excursion comes to an end, you'll carry with you a profound appreciation for the unspoiled beauty of Glacier Bay National Park. The pristine wilderness, the majestic glaciers, and the diverse wildlife have left an indelible mark on your soul. You realize that this remote corner of the world is a sanctuary for nature's wonders, a place where the forces of ice and time continue to shape the landscape, and where the harmony between the land, sea, and living creatures remains intact.

Glacier Bay National Park stands as a testament to the power and resilience of nature. It serves as a reminder of the need to protect and conserve these precious ecosystems, ensuring that future generations can continue to marvel at the beauty and splendor of this natural wonder while also understanding the delicate balance that sustains it. A journey through Glacier Bay is not just a cruise; it's an immersive experience that connects you to the raw power and magnificence of the natural world.

In conclusion, Glacier Bay National Park is an extraordinary destination that offers a once-in-a-lifetime experience for travelers. Its pristine wilderness, vast glaciers, towering mountains, and abundant wildlife create a mesmerizing tableau that captivates the senses and leaves a lasting impression. Whether you witness the calving of a glacier, spot a breaching humpback whale, or paddle through the tranquil waters in a kayak, Glacier Bay offers a profound connection to nature that is both humbling and awe-inspiring.

As you embark on your Alaska cruise, be sure to include Glacier Bay National Park in your itinerary. It is a place where the majesty of the natural world unfolds before your eyes, where the ancient forces of ice shape the landscape, and where wildlife thrives in harmony with its surroundings. Take the time to immerse yourself in the serenity of this remote wilderness, listen to the cracking of ice, feel the chill of the breeze, and witness the wonders that have been sculpted over millennia. Glacier Bay National Park is a true gem of Alaska, and it beckons you to explore its grandeur and embrace the profound connection it offers to the natural world.

5.2 Hubbard Glacier: Witnessing the Power of Ice

Located in the remote region of Yakutat, Hubbard Glacier is a monumental natural wonder that should not be missed during an Alaska cruise. This colossal glacier is the largest tidewater glacier in North America, spanning approximately 76 miles in length and standing about 300 feet tall at its face. As you approach Hubbard Glacier, you'll be greeted by an awe-inspiring landscape of towering ice walls and brilliant blue ice, immersing you in a world of frozen beauty.

One of the most captivating aspects of Hubbard Glacier is its active calving. Calving occurs when massive chunks of ice break off from the glacier's face and crash into the sea, creating a dramatic spectacle that showcases the power and majesty of the glacier. The cracking sound of the ice reverberates through the air, accompanied by the thunderous splash as the icebergs plunge into the water below. This dynamic display of nature's forces is both humbling and mesmerizing, reminding us of the constant change and transformation that occurs in the glacial landscape.

Witnessing the calving of Hubbard Glacier is an unforgettable experience that highlights the raw power and immense scale of the glacier. As you stand on the deck of your cruise ship, or in a prime viewing location specially designated for glacier viewing, you'll be able to witness this incredible natural phenomenon up close. The anticipation builds as you hear the cracks and creaks of the ice, signaling an imminent calving event. Then, with a resounding boom, a portion of the glacier breaks free, sending a cascade of ice and water into the sea. The sight is nothing short of awe-inspiring, leaving you in awe of the forces of nature.

Aside from the dramatic calving events, the sheer size of Hubbard Glacier is a sight to behold. As you approach the glacier, you'll be struck by its immensity and grandeur. The towering ice walls rise high above the water, casting a majestic shadow on the surrounding landscape. The deep blue hues of the ice create a stunning contrast against the sky and sea, showcasing the purity and clarity of the glacial ice.

Many cruise ships offer prime viewing locations on their decks, equipped with comfortable seating areas and panoramic windows, allowing you to appreciate the grandeur of Hubbard Glacier in utmost comfort. You can sip a warm drink from the onboard café or lounge, immersing yourself in the serene atmosphere as you witness the glacier's ever-changing beauty. The cruise staff often provide commentary and interesting facts about the glacier, enhancing your understanding of its formation, movement, and significance.

While the visual spectacle of Hubbard Glacier is undoubtedly the main attraction, the experience goes beyond just witnessing the power of ice. The surrounding environment offers a sense of tranquility and serenity that is hard to replicate elsewhere. The crisp air, tinged with the scent of saltwater and glacial ice, invigorates your senses. The vast expanse of ice and water creates a sense of solitude and remoteness, allowing you to disconnect from the hustle and bustle of everyday life and connect with the pristine natural world.

As you marvel at the icy landscape, you may also encounter wildlife that calls this icy realm home. Keep a lookout for seals lounging on floating icebergs or eagles soaring overhead, taking advantage of the abundant food sources that the glacier provides. The unique ecosystem surrounding Hubbard Glacier supports a diverse array of marine life, and if you're lucky, you may even spot a pod of orcas or humpback whales swimming through the icy waters.

Hubbard Glacier serves as a reminder of the importance of preserving these magnificent natural wonders. As climate change continues to impact our planet, glaciers like Hubbard are facing significant challenges. The retreating ice and changing ecosystems have far-reaching implications for the environment and the species that depend on them. By experiencing the grandeur of Hubbard Glacier firsthand, you develop a deeper appreciation for the urgency of conservation efforts and the need to protect these fragile ecosystems for future generations.

As you continue your Alaska cruise, make sure to include Hubbard Glacier in your itinerary. It is a destination that offers a rare opportunity to witness the power and beauty of ice in all its glory. Whether you're capturing stunning photographs of calving events, reflecting on the immense scale of the glacier, or simply basking in the tranquility of the surroundings, Hubbard Glacier promises an unforgettable experience that will leave a lasting impression.

 Hubbard Glacier is a natural wonder that epitomizes the sheer power and beauty of ice. Its colossal size, active calving, and breathtaking surroundings make it a must-see destination during an Alaska cruise. Witnessing the raw forces of nature at work, you'll gain a newfound appreciation for the intricate and fragile balance of our planet's ecosystems. As you stand in awe of the grandeur of Hubbard Glacier, you become part of a select group of individuals who have had the privilege of experiencing this awe-inspiring natural wonder.

5.3 Tracy Arm Fjord: Pristine Beauty and Wildlife Encounters

Nestled amidst the stunning landscapes of the Tongass National Forest, Tracy Arm Fjord is a narrow, glacier-carved fjord that offers visitors a glimpse of pristine beauty and unforgettable wildlife encounters. This scenic gem is often regarded as one of the most breathtaking destinations along an Alaska cruise, captivating the imagination with its awe-inspiring vistas and untouched wilderness.

As your ship gracefully navigates through the tranquil waters of Tracy Arm Fjord, you'll find yourself surrounded by a mesmerizing tapestry of natural wonders. Towering granite cliffs rise majestically from the fjord, creating a dramatic backdrop that seems to touch the sky. Cascading waterfalls, their streams sparkling in the sunlight, add an ethereal touch to the already enchanting scenery. The fjord is enveloped by lush emerald-green forests that stretch as far as the eye can see, creating a serene ambiance that is both soothing and invigorating.

One of the highlights of Tracy Arm Fjord is the presence of magnificent glaciers. The Sawyer Glaciers, comprised of the

Sawyer Glacier and the South Sawyer Glacier, are among the fjord's most iconic attractions. These impressive glaciers are renowned for their stunning blue hues and the dynamic calving events that occur as chunks of ice break off and plunge into the frigid waters below. The sight of these massive icebergs floating serenely in the fjord is truly awe-inspiring, serving as a testament to the immense power and ever-changing nature of glacial landscapes.

While Tracy Arm Fjord's glaciers command attention, it is the diverse array of wildlife that truly adds life and vibrancy to the fjord's pristine beauty. Harbor seals, with their soulful eyes and sleek bodies, can often be seen lounging on floating icebergs or basking on rocky outcrops. Mountain goats, agile climbers adapted to the rugged terrain, gracefully traverse the fjord's steep slopes in search of vegetation. Black bears, with their distinctive coats and lumbering gait, may emerge from the forest to forage along the shoreline, showcasing the harmonious coexistence of land and sea in this unique ecosystem.

The skies above Tracy Arm Fjord are also teeming with life. Bald eagles, with their iconic white heads and powerful wingspans, soar gracefully overhead, their keen eyes ever watchful for potential prey. Seabirds, including arctic terns and pigeon guillemots, dart through the air or dive beneath the water's surface, exhibiting their remarkable agility and adaptability to the fjord's marine environment. These avian inhabitants provide a captivating display of aerial acrobatics, further enhancing the enchanting atmosphere of Tracy Arm Fjord.

To fully immerse yourself in the beauty of Tracy Arm Fjord, many cruise ships offer small-boat excursions or guided kayak tours. These experiences allow you to get even closer to the fjord's intricate ice formations, providing an intimate and immersive encounter with its natural wonders. Gliding through the calm waters in a kayak, you'll feel a profound sense of tranquility and connection with nature. The rhythmic paddle strokes blend harmoniously with the sounds of lapping water and distant bird calls, creating a symphony of serenity.

As you explore Tracy Arm Fjord in a small boat or kayak, you'll have the opportunity to witness the intricate details of the ice formations up close. The mesmerizing patterns etched into the ice reveal the passage of time and the forces of nature that have shaped the fjord over centuries. The translucent blue hues of the ice take on an ethereal glow, captivating the senses and igniting a sense of wonder. In this intimate setting, you become part of the fjord experience, attuned to its rhythm and in harmony with its natural wonders.

Tracy Arm Fjord's allure lies not only in its breathtaking scenery and captivating wildlife but also in its untouched wilderness. The fjord remains largely unspoiled, providing a refuge for flora and fauna to thrive undisturbed. The pristine environment serves as a reminder of the importance of conservation and stewardship, inspiring a deep appreciation for the delicate balance of nature.

As you embark on a small-boat excursion or kayak tour, expert guides and naturalists will accompany you, sharing their knowledge and insights about the fjord's ecology, geology, and wildlife. They will point out the hidden wonders and fascinating stories that lie within Tracy Arm Fjord, enriching your experience and deepening your understanding of this remarkable ecosystem. Their passion and expertise will enhance your appreciation for the fjord's intricate interconnectedness and the delicate relationships that sustain life within its boundaries.

Tracy Arm Fjord offers a true escape from the demands of modern life, allowing you to disconnect from the distractions of technology and immerse yourself in the wonders of the natural world. The absence of noise pollution and the embrace of solitude create a space for introspection and reflection. It's a chance to pause, to breathe in the crisp, clean air, and to appreciate the beauty that surrounds you in its purest form.

Each visit to Tracy Arm Fjord is unique, as the fjord transforms with the changing seasons and weather conditions. Spring brings a sense of renewal as the fjord awakens from its winter slumber, with blooming wildflowers adorning the hillsides and newborn wildlife making their first appearances. Summer bathes the fjord in warmth and sunlight, illuminating the landscape with a golden glow. Autumn paints the forests in vibrant hues of red, orange, and gold, creating a breathtaking tapestry of color. Winter cloaks the fjord in a serene stillness, with snow-capped peaks and glistening ice reflecting the soft light.

Tracy Arm Fjord is a true hidden gem of Alaska's wilderness, offering a glimpse into a world of pristine beauty and remarkable wildlife encounters. It invites you to slow down, to appreciate the wonders of nature, and to reconnect with the essence of life. Whether you're standing on the deck of your cruise ship, capturing photographs of glaciers and wildlife, or gliding silently through the fjord in a kayak, Tracy Arm Fjord promises an experience that will leave an indelible mark on your soul.

Tracy Arm Fjord is a testament to the awe-inspiring power of nature and the extraordinary beauty that exists within Alaska's wilderness. Its towering granite cliffs, cascading waterfalls, and pristine forests create a backdrop of unparalleled splendor. The presence of magnificent glaciers and diverse wildlife further enriches the fjord's allure, offering a truly immersive and transformative experience for visitors. Whether you choose to explore Tracy Arm Fjord from the comfort of a cruise ship or venture closer in a small boat or kayak, you will be captivated by its pristine beauty, its tranquil ambiance, and the profound connection it fosters with the natural world. Tracy Arm Fjord is a sanctuary of serenity, an oasis of untouched wilderness that beckons you to embark on a journey of discovery and wonder.

CHAPTER SIX

Wildlife and Nature Encounters

6.1 Whale Watching: Spotting Majestic Marine Life

Alaska's coastal waters are renowned for their abundance of marine life, making it a prime destination for whale watching enthusiasts. The experience of witnessing these majestic giants of the sea in their natural habitat is nothing short of awe-inspiring, leaving a lasting impression on anyone fortunate enough to embark on an Alaska cruise.

As you set sail on your Alaska cruise, you have the opportunity to partake in whale watching activities from different vantage points. Some cruises offer specially equipped whale watching boats, designed to provide optimal viewing opportunities and ensure a comfortable and safe experience for passengers. Alternatively, you can also enjoy whale watching right from the deck of your cruise ship, which offers a unique perspective and the convenience of staying within the confines of your floating sanctuary.

Whale watching in Alaska presents a remarkable opportunity to encounter a variety of whale species, each with its own unique characteristics and behaviors. Among the most commonly spotted whale species in Alaska's coastal waters are humpback whales, orcas (also known as killer whales), and gray whales.

Humpback whales are renowned for their impressive acrobatic displays, often breaching out of the water and landing with a resounding splash. Witnessing a humpback whale breach is an awe-inspiring sight, as their massive bodies launch into the air before crashing back into the sea. These whales are also known for their distinct songs, which can be heard underwater and carry for long distances. The expert naturalists and guides on board your cruise ship will provide fascinating insights into the behaviors and biology of humpback whales, enhancing your understanding and appreciation of these incredible creatures.

Orcas, or killer whales, are another highlight of Alaska's whale watching experience. These intelligent and social creatures are known for their striking black and white coloration and their remarkable hunting strategies. Orcas often travel in tightly-knit family pods, working together to hunt and communicate using a complex system of clicks, whistles, and calls. Observing orcas in their natural environment is a captivating experience, as you witness their synchronized movements and interactions within the pod. The knowledgeable guides accompanying you on your whale watching excursion will share their expertise on orca behavior, shedding light on the intricacies of their social structure and hunting techniques.

Gray whales, although less acrobatic than humpback whales, captivate onlookers with their sheer size and gentle nature. Known for their epic annual migration from the Bering Sea to the warm waters of Mexico, gray whales undertake one of the longest migrations of any mammal on Earth. Along the coast of Alaska, you may have the privilege of spotting these magnificent creatures as they travel through the rich feeding grounds of the region. With their mottled gray skin and distinctive heart-shaped blow, gray whales are a sight to behold. Expert naturalists will provide valuable insights into their migration patterns and feeding habits, allowing you to gain a deeper understanding of their remarkable journey.

As you embark on your whale watching adventure, the presence of expert naturalists and guides on board your Alaska cruise ensures a truly educational and unforgettable experience. These knowledgeable individuals possess a wealth of information about the marine life in Alaska's coastal waters, and they are dedicated to sharing their passion and expertise with cruise passengers.

During your whale watching excursions, the naturalists will provide valuable insights into the behaviors, biology, and conservation efforts related to these incredible animals. You will learn about the life cycles of different whale species, their feeding habits, mating rituals, and the challenges they face in their marine environment. This educational aspect of whale watching adds a deeper layer of appreciation and respect for these magnificent creatures, inspiring a sense of environmental stewardship.

Beyond the thrill of spotting whales, your whale watching adventure in Alaska offers a unique opportunity to immerse yourself in the natural wonders of the region. The expansive coastal waters, framed by snow-capped mountains and rugged coastline, create a picturesque backdrop for your whale watching endeavors. As you scan the horizon for signs of marine life, you'll also have the chance to appreciate the breathtaking beauty of Alaska's landscapes.

The anticipation builds as you keep your eyes peeled for the telltale signs of whale activity. Suddenly, a burst of water erupts from the surface, followed by the graceful emergence of a humpback whale's enormous fluke. The sight leaves you in awe as you marvel at the power and grace of these magnificent creatures. The naturalists on board will help identify the different behaviors exhibited by the whales, such as breaching, tail slapping, and spy-hopping, providing insights into their communication and survival strategies.

The importance of responsible whale watching practices is emphasized throughout your Alaska cruise. The naturalists and guides prioritize the well-being of the whales and their natural habitat, ensuring that their interactions with these animals are respectful and minimally intrusive. By maintaining a safe distance and adhering to guidelines for whale watching, you contribute to the preservation of these fragile ecosystems and help protect the whales from unnecessary disturbances.

Whale watching in Alaska extends beyond mere observation; it also serves as a platform for scientific research and conservation efforts. Many cruise ships participate in citizen science programs, allowing passengers to contribute to ongoing research projects by recording whale sightings and behaviors. By engaging in these initiatives, you actively participate in the broader understanding of whale populations, migratory patterns, and the overall health of the marine environment.

As your whale watching adventure comes to an end, the memories and emotions evoked by your encounters with these magnificent creatures remain etched in your mind. The beauty and grandeur of Alaska's coastal waters, combined with the remarkable behaviors of the whales, create a profound connection with the natural world. The experience serves as a reminder of the importance of preserving these delicate ecosystems and the incredible biodiversity they support.

In addition to whale watching, your Alaska cruise offers a plethora of other wildlife encounters and nature exploration opportunities. From bear watching to birdwatching and exploring Alaska's national parks and reserves, there is an abundance of experiences awaiting you.

6.2 Bear Watching: Observing Alaska's Iconic Predators

Alaska's population of bears is legendary, and bear watching is a thrilling and unforgettable activity that allows you to witness these iconic predators in their natural habitat. As you embark on your Alaska cruise, you'll have the opportunity to explore coastal areas and river estuaries, where bears gather in large numbers to feast on the abundant salmon runs that occur during the summer months. These prime bear viewing locations offer a glimpse into the lives of both the brown bear, including the famous coastal grizzly bear, and the black bear, two of the most commonly encountered bear species in Alaska.

Guided excursions led by experienced naturalists will be a highlight of your bear watching adventure. These experts possess in-depth knowledge of bear behavior and are well-versed in the safety protocols necessary for observing bears in the wild. They will take you to carefully selected locations, ensuring your safety while maximizing your chances of spotting these impressive creatures. With their guidance, you'll be able to observe bears from a safe distance, allowing you to witness their fishing techniques, playfulness, and interactions with other wildlife.

The brown bear, also known as the grizzly bear, is a majestic species that has come to symbolize the untamed wilderness of Alaska. These massive creatures can weigh up to 1,500 pounds and possess an imposing presence. Coastal areas and river estuaries serve as prime locations for observing brown bears, as they gather in large numbers to take advantage of the abundant salmon runs that occur during the summer months. Guided excursions will take you to these areas, where you'll witness the bears' fishing techniques as they employ their strength and agility to catch their prized prey. You may observe bears patiently waiting in the water, using their powerful paws to snatch salmon from the rushing currents. The naturalists accompanying you will provide valuable insights into the behavior and biology of brown bears, enhancing your understanding and appreciation of these magnificent creatures.

Black bears, while smaller in size compared to brown bears, are equally captivating to observe. These bears can be found in various habitats throughout Alaska, including forested areas and even urban environments. While their name may suggest a singular color, black bears can actually range in color from black to brown, blond, or cinnamon. During your bear watching excursions, with the guidance of knowledgeable naturalists, you may be fortunate enough to catch a glimpse of these remarkable creatures as they forage for berries or navigate their territory. Observing black bears in their natural habitat offers a unique opportunity to witness their resourcefulness and adaptability, as they navigate the challenges of finding food and avoiding potential threats.

Bear watching in Alaska is not only a thrilling activity but also an opportunity to gain a deeper appreciation for the vital role bears play in the state's ecosystem. Bears are considered keystone species, meaning their presence and activities have a significant impact on the balance and health of their habitats. They contribute to seed dispersal, nutrient cycling, and the regulation of prey populations. By observing bears in their natural environment, you'll gain a better understanding of the complex interconnections between bears, salmon, other wildlife, and the overall ecosystem. The naturalists accompanying you on your excursions will share their expertise on the ecological significance of bears and the conservation efforts aimed at ensuring their survival.

Responsible bear watching practices are essential to minimize disturbances and ensure the well-being of both the bears and their natural habitats. Your naturalist guides will emphasize the importance of maintaining a safe distance and respecting the bears' space. This approach ensures that your interactions with these magnificent creatures are respectful and minimally intrusive, allowing them to carry out their natural behaviors undisturbed. By adhering to the guidelines and following the instructions of the naturalists, you contribute to the preservation of these fragile ecosystems and help protect the bears from unnecessary stress.

Bear watching in Alaska offers a unique opportunityto witness the power, beauty, and intricate behaviors of these remarkable creatures. It is an experience that will leave you with a profound appreciation for the delicate balance of nature and the need to protect these majestic animals and their habitats.

As you embark on your Alaska cruise and venture into the coastal waters, you'll be entering the realm of some of the world's most awe-inspiring marine life. Whale watching becomes a highlight of your journey, as you keep your eyes peeled for the magnificent giants of the sea. The most commonly spotted whale species in Alaska include humpback whales, orcas (also known as killer whales), and gray whales.

Humpback whales are known for their acrobatic displays, often breaching the surface and splashing back into the water with incredible force. Their long pectoral fins, or flippers, create a distinctive sight as they slap the water, generating powerful splashes. Witnessing these awe-inspiring behaviors leaves you in awe of the humpback whales' power and grace.

Orcas, with their striking black and white markings, are also a sight to behold. These highly intelligent and social creatures are known for their complex hunting techniques and vocalizations. Observing orcas as they travel in family groups, communicate with each other, and hunt their prey provides a unique window into their social dynamics and sophisticated behaviors.

Gray whales, on the other hand, are known for their long migrations. These gentle giants undertake one of the longest known migrations of any mammal, traveling thousands of miles between their feeding grounds in Alaska and their breeding grounds in Mexico. Witnessing the spectacle of gray whales as they navigate the coastal waters of Alaska is a testament to their endurance and resilience.

During your whale watching adventure, expert naturalists and guides on board your cruise ship will provide valuable insights into the behaviors and biology of these incredible animals. They will share their knowledge about the whales' migration patterns, feeding habits, and conservation status, enriching your experience and deepening your understanding of the marine ecosystem.

Whale watching in Alaska is not only a thrilling and educational experience, but it also carries a deeper significance. It serves as a reminder of the importance of protecting these magnificent creatures and their habitats. Whales play a crucial role in maintaining the health of the oceans and the delicate balance of marine ecosystems. Their feeding habits, migration patterns, and interactions with other species contribute to the overall biodiversity and productivity of the marine environment.

By observing whales in their natural habitat and learning about their behaviors, we develop a deeper appreciation for their role as keystone species and the need to protect their habitats.

During your bear watching excursions, you'll learn about the various bear behaviors and communication techniques. Bears have intricate social structures and hierarchies, and observing their interactions can be a fascinating experience. You might witness cubs playing under the watchful eye of their mother or male bears asserting dominance over their territory. These moments provide a glimpse into the complex lives of bears and highlight the importance of preserving their natural habitats.

To ensure a safe and respectful bear watching experience, it is crucial to follow the guidance of your naturalist guides. They will educate you on maintaining a safe distance and avoiding any actions that could disturb or endanger the bears. Respecting their space and observing from a distance allows you to witness their natural behaviors without causing unnecessary stress or disruption.

Bear watching in Alaska also offers opportunities to contribute to bear research and conservation efforts. Many cruise companies partner with local organizations and wildlife agencies to gather data and monitor bear populations. As a participant in these initiatives, you may have the chance to assist in data collection, such as recording bear sightings and behaviors. By contributing to these research projects, you actively contribute to the understanding and conservation of Alaska's bears.

Beyond the bears themselves, the landscapes that serve as their habitats are equally stunning. Alaska's coastal areas and river estuaries provide a backdrop of rugged beauty, where bears roam freely in search of food. The vastness of the wilderness and the pristine nature of the surroundings create a sense of awe and wonder as you witness these creatures in their natural element. The towering mountains, dense forests, and shimmering waters combine to form a landscape that is as breathtaking as the bears themselves.

Bear watching in Alaska is not only a thrilling activity, but it also carries important ecological and conservation significance. Bears play a crucial role in maintaining the balance of ecosystems, particularly through their interactions with salmon. Salmon runs are a vital part of the Alaskan ecosystem, as they bring essential nutrients from the ocean to the inland areas. Bears, in their pursuit of salmon, contribute to the dispersal of these nutrients, helping to fertilize the surrounding landscapes and support a diverse array of flora and fauna.

The presence of bears also acts as an indicator of the overall health of the ecosystem. Their populations are directly influenced by the availability of food, the quality of habitats, and the presence of other wildlife species. By monitoring bear populations and studying their behaviors, scientists and conservationists gain valuable insights into the state of the environment and can implement measures to protect these invaluable habitats.

Engaging in responsible bear watching practices is paramount to ensure the well-being of both the bears and their habitats. It is essential to follow the guidelines and instructions provided by your naturalist guides. These guidelines often include maintaining a safe distance, avoiding sudden movements or loud noises, and refraining from feeding or approaching the bears. By adhering to these practices, you minimize disturbances and allow the bears to carry out their natural behaviors undisturbed.

The opportunity to observe bears in their natural habitat is a privilege that comes with a responsibility to protect and conserve these magnificent creatures and the ecosystems they inhabit. Supporting local conservation initiatives, participating in educational programs, and advocating for responsible tourism practices are ways to contribute to the long-term preservation of Alaska's bears and their habitats.

In conclusion, Alaska's coastal waters offer a unique and awe-inspiring opportunity for bear watching during your cruise. Witnessing the power, grace, and natural behaviors of bears in their natural habitat is an experience that will leave a lasting impression. Guided by experienced naturalists, you'll explore prime bear viewing locations and gain valuable insights into the behaviors and ecological significance of these iconic predators. By adhering to responsible bear watching practices and supporting conservation efforts, you play a vital role in preserving these majestic creatures and the pristine wilderness they call home. Bear watching in Alaska is not just an adventure; it's an opportunity to connect with nature, deepen your understanding of the natural world, and foster a sense of stewardship for the protection of these incredible animals.

6.3 Birdwatching: Discovering Avian Diversity

Alaska's vast and varied landscapes provide a haven for bird enthusiasts and offer a treasure trove of avian diversity. As you embark on your Alaska cruise, prepare to be captivated by the incredible array of bird species that inhabit the state's forests, wetlands, and coastal areas. Birdwatching in Alaska is an extraordinary experience that allows you to witness the beauty and wonder of both resident and migratory birds in their natural habitats.

One of the most iconic birds of Alaska is the bald eagle, a symbol of strength and majesty. These magnificent birds can be spotted throughout the state, soaring through the skies or perched on tree branches near bodies of water. Keep your eyes peeled for their distinctive white heads and dark brown bodies as they scan the surroundings for fish or carrion. Witnessing the graceful flight of bald eagles against the backdrop of Alaska's breathtaking landscapes is a sight that will leave you in awe.

Another highlight of birdwatching in Alaska is the opportunity to observe puffins, seabirds renowned for their colorful beaks and distinctive appearance. The waters surrounding Alaska are home to several species of puffins, including the tufted puffin and the horned puffin. These charming birds can often be seen bobbing on the surface of the water or perched on rocky cliffs, where they nest and raise their young. Their comical antics and vibrant plumage make them a delight to watch and photograph.

Arctic terns are also a common sight in Alaska and hold the remarkable distinction of having the longest migration of any bird species. These graceful birds travel incredible distances, flying from their breeding grounds in the Arctic to their wintering grounds in the Antarctic and back again. Witnessing the swift and agile flight of arctic terns as they traverse the Alaskan skies is a testament to their endurance and navigational abilities.

Coastal areas of Alaska are teeming with a wide variety of seabirds, each with its own unique characteristics and behaviors. Cormorants, with their sleek bodies and distinctive hooked beaks, are often seen perched on rocks, drying their wings after a fishing expedition. These skilled divers can disappear beneath the surface for extended periods, emerging with fish in their beaks.

Seabird colonies in Alaska are also home to a diverse array of other species, including guillemots, murres, and kittiwakes. These seabirds form bustling colonies on rocky cliffs and islands, creating a cacophony of calls and activity. Observing these colonies during the nesting season offers a rare opportunity to witness the social dynamics and breeding behaviors of these fascinating birds.

Inland areas of Alaska provide habitats for a variety of land birds, each adapted to the unique environments they inhabit. Spruce grouse, with their mottled brown plumage, are often found in the dense forests, blending seamlessly with their surroundings. Black-capped chickadees, known for their cheerful songs and playful demeanor, flit through the trees, captivating observers with their acrobatic flights. Varied thrushes, with their vibrant orange and black plumage, add a splash of color to the forest understory as they forage for insects and berries.

Experienced birdwatching guides will accompany you on excursions, sharing their knowledge and expertise to help you identify and appreciate the distinct behaviors and characteristics of each species. They will point out the subtle details that distinguish one bird from another, helping you develop a deeper understanding of the avian world.

To enhance your birdwatching experience, be sure to bring binoculars and a camera. Binoculars allow you to observe birds from a distance without disturbing their natural behaviors. The ability to see fine details, such as the intricate patterns on a bird's feathers or the subtle nuances of its behavior, adds a new dimension to your birdwatching adventure. A camera enables you to capture stunning images of these feathered wonders, creating lasting memories of your encounters with Alaska's avian inhabitants.

As you immerse yourself in the world of birdwatching, you'll also gain a greater appreciation for the interconnectedness of ecosystems and the role that birds play in maintaining the balance of nature. Birds serve as pollinators, seed dispersers, and indicators of ecosystem health. Their migrations connect distant habitats, spreading nutrients and contributing to the survival of plants and other wildlife. By observing and studying birds, scientists can gather valuable information about the state of the environment and implement conservation measures to protect these delicate ecosystems.

In addition to the joy of observing birds in their natural habitats, birdwatching in Alaska offers a sense of tranquility and connection with nature. The untouched wilderness, vast expanses of forests, and pristine coastal areas create a serene backdrop for your birdwatching adventures. The peacefulness of these environments allows you to immerse yourself in the sights and sounds of nature, providing a welcome respite from the hustle and bustle of everyday life.

During your Alaska cruise, take advantage of the various birdwatching opportunities offered by your itinerary. Guided excursions to prime birdwatching locations will allow you to explore diverse habitats and encounter a wide range of bird species. Whether you find yourself on a secluded beach, a lush rainforest trail, or a rocky cliff overlooking the ocean, be prepared to be amazed by the avian wonders that await you.

As you venture into the world of birdwatching, remember to practice responsible wildlife viewing. Respect the natural habitats of the birds and observe from a distance to avoid causing disturbance. Follow the guidance of your guides and adhere to any specific regulations or guidelines provided. By being mindful of your impact and respecting the birds' needs, you can ensure a positive and sustainable birdwatching experience.

In conclusion, birdwatching during your Alaska cruise is a captivating and rewarding experience. The state's diverse landscapes provide habitats for a wide range of bird species, offering bird enthusiasts an opportunity to observe rare and migratory birds in their natural surroundings. From the majestic bald eagles to the comical puffins and the graceful arctic terns, Alaska's avian inhabitants never fail to impress with their beauty and behaviors. With the assistance of knowledgeable guides and the aid of binoculars and a camera, you'll be able to fully appreciate the intricate details and unique characteristics of each species. Moreover, birdwatching in Alaska fosters a deeper understanding of the interconnectedness of ecosystems and the need to protect and preserve these habitats for future generations. So, set forth on your birdwatching adventure, embrace the serenity of nature, and let the feathered wonders of Alaska inspire and uplift your spirit.

6.4 Exploring Alaska's National Parks and Reserves

Alaska's national parks and reserves are the crown jewels of its wilderness, offering a gateway to some of the most spectacular landscapes and wildlife encounters on Earth. These protected areas showcase the raw beauty and untamed wilderness that make Alaska a destination of unparalleled allure. During your Alaska cruise, you'll have the opportunity to immerse yourself in the awe-inspiring grandeur of these iconic parks, each with its own unique offerings and experiences.

Denali National Park, home to the towering Denali, North America's highest peak, is a place of superlatives. As you venture into the heart of this pristine wilderness, you'll be greeted by a tapestry of untouched landscapes. Vast expanses of tundra, majestic mountain ranges, and meandering rivers create a backdrop that is both humbling and enchanting. Guided hikes through alpine meadows reveal a kaleidoscope of wildflowers and an array of wildlife, including grizzly bears, moose, caribou, and Dall sheep. The sheer scale and untouched beauty of Denali National Park will leave you in awe, as you witness the untamed spirit of Alaska unfold before your eyes.

Kenai Fjords National Park offers a captivating blend of ice, ocean, and rugged coastline. This maritime wilderness is characterized by its deep fjords, tidewater glaciers, and abundant marine life. Gliding through the icy waters on a boat tour, you'll witness the grandeur of massive glaciers calving into the sea, sending thunderous cracks and splashes reverberating through the air. Keep your eyes peeled for humpback whales breaching, sea otters frolicking in kelp forests, and seabirds nesting on rocky cliffs. Exploring the labyrinthine waterways and hidden coves of Kenai Fjords National Park is a mesmerizing experience that connects you intimately with the power and beauty of Alaska's coastal wilderness.

Glacier Bay National Park is a UNESCO World Heritage Site that showcases the dynamic relationship between glaciers and the surrounding ecosystem. This living laboratory provides a front-row seat to witness the ever-changing landscape shaped by ice. As you sail through the bay's icy waters, you'll encounter tidewater glaciers that stretch as far as the eye can see. The dramatic calving of icebergs, the thunderous rumble of glacial movement, and the ethereal blue hues of the ice create a spectacle that is nothing short of breathtaking. While exploring Glacier Bay, you'll have the chance to spot marine mammals such as seals and sea lions, as well as a variety of seabirds that call this icy realm home.

Wrangell-St. Elias National Park, the largest national park in the United States, is a land of superlatives and superlatives. Its vast expanses encompass towering peaks, sprawling glaciers, and remote wilderness. Here, you can embark on epic adventures, such as trekking on ancient glaciers, hiking through alpine valleys, or rafting down wild rivers. The park's rich biodiversity supports a variety of wildlife, including wolves, wolverines, and the elusive mountain goats that effortlessly navigate the rugged cliffs. Wrangell-St. Elias offers a true wilderness experience that will ignite your sense of adventure and leave you with a profound appreciation for the power and resilience of nature.

Guided excursions within these national parks and reserves provide invaluable insights into the history, geology, and ecology of these remarkable landscapes. Expert naturalist guides will accompany you, sharing their knowledge and deep appreciation for the region, ensuring you have a meaningful and informative experience.

As you explore these pristine wilderness areas, it is crucial to respect and preserve their delicate ecosystems. Follow the Leave No Trace principles, stay on designated trails, and minimize your impact on the environment. By treading lightly and practicing responsible tourism, you canhelp protect these incredible landscapes for future generations to enjoy.

In addition to the stunning natural beauty, Alaska's national parks and reserves offer opportunities for cultural exploration. The land within these protected areas holds great significance for indigenous communities, who have inhabited these territories for thousands of years. Many guided excursions provide insights into the rich cultural heritage of Alaska's native peoples, sharing stories, traditions, and knowledge that have been passed down through generations. This cultural exchange adds a layer of depth and understanding to your journey, fostering a greater appreciation for the interconnectedness of nature and human history.

The experience of exploring Alaska's national parks and reserves goes beyond sightseeing. It's about forging a connection with the land, immersing yourself in its rhythms, and experiencing the sense of wonder that only wild places can evoke. Each park has its own distinct character, offering a tapestry of experiences that range from serene contemplation to adrenaline-pumping adventures. Whether you choose to hike along a meandering trail, paddle through pristine waterways, or simply stand in awe of the magnificent vistas, Alaska's national parks and reserves are bound to leave an indelible mark on your soul.

To make the most of your time in these wilderness havens, it's important to come prepared. Dress in layers to adapt to the ever-changing weather conditions, wear sturdy footwear for exploring rugged terrains, and carry essential supplies such as water, snacks, and sunscreen. Listen attentively to your guides, who are not only knowledgeable about the flora, fauna, and geology but also serve as stewards of these precious landscapes.

Remember that while visiting these national parks and reserves is an extraordinary privilege, it also comes with the responsibility to conserve and protect these environments. Embrace the principles of responsible tourism, such as minimizing waste, respecting wildlife and their habitats, and supporting local conservation efforts. By leaving a positive impact on the places you visit, you contribute to the preservation of Alaska's natural heritage.

Exploring Alaska's national parks and reserves during your cruise is an opportunity to delve into the heart of true wilderness. Denali, Kenai Fjords, Glacier Bay, and Wrangell-

St. Elias beckon with their untamed beauty, showcasing the remarkable diversity and resilience of Alaska's ecosystems. Through guided excursions, you'll uncover the secrets of these landscapes, encountering towering mountains, icy glaciers, and vibrant wildlife along the way. As you stand in awe of nature's grandeur, remember to tread gently, respecting the delicate balance of these ecosystems and appreciating the rich cultural heritage intertwined with the land. Let Alaska's national parks and reserves be a source of inspiration, rejuvenation, and a reminder of the importance of preserving our natural treasures.

CHAPTER SEVEN

Cultural Highlights of Alaska

7.1 Indigenous Cultures: Learning about Alaska's Native Peoples

Alaska is home to a rich tapestry of indigenous cultures, each with its distinct traditions, languages, and history. In this chapter, we delve into the fascinating world of Alaska's Native peoples, providing insights into their vibrant cultures and deep connections with the land and sea.

Cultural Diversity: Alaska is a land rich in cultural diversity, and its indigenous peoples have inhabited the region for thousands of years. The state is home to a wide array of Native groups, each with its distinct heritage, languages, and traditions. Let's delve deeper into some of the diverse Native groups of Alaska:

- Inupiaq: The Inupiaq people are primarily located in the northern and northwestern parts of Alaska, including the North Slope and Bering Strait regions. They have a strong connection to the Arctic environment and rely on subsistence hunting, fishing, and whaling. Inupiaq culture encompasses intricate

skin sewing, storytelling, and a deep spiritual relationship with nature.
- Yup'ik: The Yup'ik people primarily reside in southwestern Alaska, particularly along the Yukon and Kuskokwim Rivers and the coastal areas. They have a rich artistic tradition, including intricately carved masks, ceremonial dance regalia, and exquisite basketry. Yup'ik culture emphasizes the importance of community, subsistence hunting and fishing, and a harmonious relationship with the natural world.
- Athabascan: The Athabascan peoples have a widespread presence throughout interior and southeastern Alaska. They comprise numerous distinct groups, such as the Gwich'in, Tanana, and Ahtna. Athabascan cultures are characterized by a strong spiritual connection to the land and rivers, with subsistence activities like hunting, trapping, and gathering playing a significant role. Traditional practices, such as beading, birch bark basketry, and storytelling, continue to be celebrated.
- Tlingit: The Tlingit people primarily inhabit the southeastern coastal regions of Alaska, including the Inside Passage. Known for their rich artistic heritage, the Tlingit are renowned for their totem pole carving, intricate Chilkat weaving, and cedar bark basketry. Their social structure is organized around clans, and they have a profound spiritual relationship with the land, sea, and animals.
- Haida: The Haida people are primarily found in the southernmost parts of the southeastern Alaska and British Columbia's Haida Gwaii archipelago. Haida culture is celebrated for its exceptional totem poles,

cedar dugout canoes, and skilled artisans in wood and argillite carving. The Haida have a deep connection to the ocean, engaging in fishing, whaling, and gathering marine resources.

These are just a few examples of the diverse Native groups in Alaska, and there are numerous other tribes and communities, each with its unique traditions and contributions to the cultural fabric of the state. By learning about their customs, spiritual beliefs, and traditional practices, you gain a deeper appreciation for the enduring heritage that has been passed down through generations. From storytelling and art to subsistence practices and language preservation, the indigenous peoples of Alaska continue to contribute to the vibrant tapestry of the Last Frontier's cultural identity.

Traditional Arts and Crafts:

The artistic expressions of Alaska's indigenous cultures are a testament to the rich cultural heritage and creative spirit that has thrived for generations. From the intricate beadwork to the stunning basketry, the art forms of Alaska's indigenous peoples reflect their deep connection to the land, their history, and their spiritual beliefs. Let's explore some of these remarkable artistic traditions:

- Beadwork: Alaska's Native artists have mastered the art of beadwork, creating intricate designs using vibrant colors and a variety of materials, including glass beads, quills, and shells. These beads are skillfully sewn onto clothing, accessories, and

ceremonial regalia, forming stunning patterns that tell stories and represent cultural symbolism.
- Basketry: Basketry holds a significant place in Alaska's indigenous cultures. Native artisans weave baskets using traditional techniques passed down through generations. These baskets showcase a harmonious blend of form and function, ranging from finely woven utilitarian baskets for gathering and storage to intricately designed decorative pieces that incorporate natural materials like spruce roots, grasses, and dyed fibers.
- Carvings: Carving is another prominent art form within Alaska's indigenous cultures. Skilled carvers shape wood, bone, and antler into intricate sculptures, masks, totem poles, and decorative objects. Totem poles, in particular, are towering masterpieces that narrate stories, commemorate ancestors, and represent the rich mythology and history of Native communities.
- Ceremonial Regalia: Alaska's indigenous cultures have a rich tradition of creating ceremonial regalia, which includes intricately crafted headdresses, dance aprons, masks, and ceremonial garments. These regalia pieces are often adorned with feathers, shells, beads, and intricate designs, symbolizing the spiritual connection and cultural significance of ceremonial practices.
- Skin Sewing: Skin sewing is a traditional art form practiced by Alaska's indigenous peoples, particularly in the Arctic regions. Using materials such as seal, walrus, or caribou skin, artisans skillfully create garments, mittens, boots, and bags, embellishing

them with decorative stitching and intricate designs. Skin sewing not only showcases the practicality of traditional clothing but also serves as a beautiful expression of cultural identity.

Through these artistic expressions, Alaska's indigenous cultures preserve their traditions, stories, and ancestral knowledge. Each piece of art reflects the skill, creativity, and dedication of Native artisans, capturing the essence of their cultural heritage. By appreciating these traditional crafts, we gain a deeper understanding of the cultural significance and artistic legacy that continue to thrive in Alaska's indigenous communities.

Cultural Centers and Museums:

Uncovering the wealth of knowledge and artifacts preserved in Alaska's indigenous cultural centers and museums is an enlightening experience that allows visitors to delve into the rich history and heritage of Native peoples. These institutions serve as gateways to understanding and appreciating the depth and diversity of Alaska's indigenous cultures. Let's explore the captivating offerings of these cultural centers and museums:

- Artifact Collections: Indigenous cultural centers and museums house extensive collections of artifacts that have been carefully preserved and curated. These collections feature a wide range of items, including traditional clothing, tools, ceremonial objects, artwork, and historical photographs. Exploring these artifacts provides a tangible connection to the past

and offers insights into the daily lives, rituals, and artistic traditions of Alaska's indigenous peoples.
- Interactive Exhibits: Cultural centers and museums often feature interactive exhibits that engage visitors in a hands-on exploration of indigenous cultures. Through multimedia displays, immersive environments, and interactive technologies, visitors can gain a deeper understanding of traditional practices, historical events, and contemporary issues faced by Native communities. Interactive exhibits may include demonstrations of traditional crafts, virtual reality experiences, and storytelling sessions that bring Native history and heritage to life.
- Performances and Demonstrations: Many cultural centers and museums showcase live performances and demonstrations by Native artists, musicians, dancers, and storytellers. These captivating presentations provide an opportunity to witness traditional songs, dances, and storytelling techniques firsthand. Through performances, visitors can experience the vibrancy and cultural expressions that have been passed down through generations, gaining a deeper appreciation for the vitality of indigenous traditions.
- Educational Programs: Indigenous cultural centers and museums offer a range of educational programs designed to promote understanding and awareness of Native history and heritage. These programs may include guided tours, workshops, lectures, and community events. Visitors can engage in hands-on activities, learn traditional skills, and participate in discussions that foster a deeper appreciation for

indigenous cultures and their ongoing contributions to the fabric of Alaskan society.
- Collaboration with Native Communities: Cultural centers and museums often work closely with Native communities to ensure that their narratives and perspectives are accurately represented. These collaborations help to ensure that the exhibits and programs reflect the lived experiences, values, and aspirations of Alaska's indigenous peoples. Through these partnerships, visitors can gain a more authentic and nuanced understanding of Native history and culture.

By visiting indigenous cultural centers and museums, visitors can immerse themselves in the rich tapestry of Alaska's indigenous heritage. These institutions offer a platform for Native voices to be heard, celebrate the resilience of indigenous communities, and foster cultural understanding and appreciation. Through the interactive exhibits, performances, and educational programs offered, visitors can embark on a transformative journey of discovery, leaving with a deeper understanding of the intricate histories and vibrant cultures that define Alaska's indigenous peoples.

Cultural Demonstrations:

Attending cultural demonstrations and events in Alaska provides a unique opportunity to witness the richness and vibrancy of Native cultures firsthand. These gatherings are immersive experiences that allow visitors to engage with traditional dances, storytelling, and drumming, creating a memorable encounter with Alaska's indigenous heritage.

Let's explore the captivating aspects of these cultural demonstrations and events:

- Traditional Dances: Native dances are a captivating showcase of Alaska's indigenous cultures. Attendees can witness the graceful movements, intricate footwork, and vibrant regalia as dancers bring to life age-old traditions. Each dance carries its unique significance, often reflecting stories, seasons, or ceremonial events. The rhythmic beats of drums and accompanying songs create an enchanting atmosphere, immersing spectators in the cultural expressions of Alaska's Native peoples.
- Storytelling: Storytelling is an integral part of Native cultures, passing down ancestral knowledge, legends, and historical accounts through generations. Cultural demonstrations and events often feature storytellers who captivate audiences with their oral traditions. These stories are not only entertaining but also carry deep cultural and spiritual meanings, providing insights into the values, beliefs, and heritage of Alaska's indigenous communities.
- Drumming and Singing: The rhythmic beats of drums and the harmonious voices of singers resonate through cultural demonstrations and events. Drumming holds a central place in Native cultures, symbolizing unity, connection, and celebration. The powerful sound of drums, combined with soul-stirring vocal performances, creates an immersive experience that evokes a sense of awe and appreciation for the musical traditions of Alaska's indigenous peoples.

- Regalia and Artistry: Cultural demonstrations and events often showcase the intricate artistry and craftsmanship of Alaska's Native communities. Attendees have the opportunity to admire the detailed work on ceremonial regalia, including headdresses, dance aprons, masks, and other traditional attire. The regalia serves as a visual representation of cultural pride and identity, reflecting the skill and creativity of Native artisans.
- Community Celebration: These events are more than just performances; they are vibrant community celebrations. They provide a space for Alaska's indigenous communities to come together, reconnect, and celebrate their shared heritage. Visitors can witness the joy and sense of belonging as community members share their traditions, fostering a sense of unity and pride.

By attending cultural demonstrations and events, visitors can experience the authenticity and vitality of Alaska's Native cultures. Immersed in the sights and sounds of traditional dances, storytelling, and drumming, attendees gain a deeper appreciation for the rich traditions, resilience, and contributions of Alaska's indigenous peoples. These experiences foster cultural understanding, promote cross-cultural connections, and create lasting memories of the vibrant tapestry of Native heritage in Alaska.

Respectful Cultural Interactions:

When engaging with Alaska's Native communities, it is essential to approach interactions with respect, cultural sensitivity, and a genuine desire to learn and appreciate their traditions. Understanding the importance of respectful cultural interactions can help foster meaningful connections and promote positive exchanges. Here are some insights into proper etiquette, protocols, and the significance of honoring Native traditions and customs:

Educate Yourself: Prior to engaging with Alaska's Native communities, take the time to educate yourself about their specific cultural practices, protocols, and history. Learn about the diverse Native groups, their traditional territories, and the issues they face today. Familiarize yourself with cultural norms, such as greetings, forms of address, and appropriate behavior in sacred or ceremonial spaces. This knowledge demonstrates your genuine interest in and respect for their culture.

Seek Permission and Consent: When visiting Native communities or participating in cultural events, it is important to seek permission and obtain consent before taking photographs, recordings, or sharing personal stories. Understand that certain ceremonies or cultural practices may be private or sacred, and photography or documentation may not be allowed. Always ask for permission and respect their wishes if they decline.

Listen and Learn: Engage in active listening and be open to learning from Native community members. Respect their expertise and knowledge as they share their stories, histories, and cultural perspectives. Avoid making assumptions or imposing your own beliefs or preconceptions. Instead, approach conversations with curiosity, humility, and a genuine willingness to learn.

Respect Personal Space and Boundaries: Be mindful of personal space and boundaries when interacting with Native community members. Recognize that cultural practices and individual preferences may vary. Allow individuals to dictate their level of comfort and avoid touching someone's regalia, ceremonial objects, or traditional attire without explicit permission.

Honor Elders and Community Leaders: In many Native communities, elders and community leaders hold significant wisdom and cultural authority. Show respect and deference to elders by listening attentively and acknowledging their knowledge and experience. When appropriate, seek their guidance or ask for their insights on cultural matters.

Support Indigenous Businesses and Artisans: Show your support for Alaska's Native communities by purchasing authentic indigenous artwork, crafts, and products from local businesses and artisans. This helps to sustain traditional practices and provide economic empowerment within Native communities.

Practice Cultural Sensitivity Online: When sharing information or engaging in discussions about Alaska's Native cultures online, exercise cultural sensitivity and avoid appropriating or misrepresenting their traditions. Be cautious with sharing sensitive or sacred information without appropriate context or permissions.

By following these guidelines, you can engage with Alaska's Native communities in a respectful and meaningful manner. Honoring their traditions, customs, and protocols demonstrates your appreciation for their cultural heritage, fosters positive cross-cultural connections, and contributes to a more inclusive and mutually beneficial relationship. Remember, cultural understanding is an ongoing journey, and approaching it with respect and humility is key to building meaningful and lasting connections with Alaska's Native communities.

7.2 Totem Poles: Artistic Expressions of Native Heritage

Totem poles are iconic symbols of Alaska's Native heritage and serve as visual storytellers, conveying ancestral legends, clan histories, and spiritual beliefs. In this section, we explore the captivating world of totem poles and their significance within Alaska's indigenous cultures.

Origins and Symbolism: Delving into the history and origins of totem poles is a fascinating journey that takes us back thousands of years and unravels the intricate symbolism embedded within these majestic structures. Totem poles hold great cultural and artistic significance for Alaska's Native communities, serving as visual narratives that represent the rich tapestry of Native culture and heritage. Let's explore the captivating world of totem poles and the meanings they convey:

- Origins and Cultural Significance: Totem poles have a long history in the indigenous cultures of Alaska, with their origins dating back thousands of years. They are monumental sculptures carved from large trees, typically cedar, and serve as important cultural markers and artistic expressions. Totem poles are created to honor ancestors, commemorate significant events, tell stories, assert clan identities, and convey spiritual beliefs.

- Symbolism and Iconography: Each totem pole is a unique work of art that tells a story through its carefully crafted symbols and iconography. Animals, mythical creatures, and ancestral figures are intricately carved into the wood, each representing different aspects of Native culture. For example, the Raven symbolizes creativity and transformation, the Bear represents strength and protection, and the Eagle embodies spiritual power and vision. These symbols come together to create a visual language that communicates the cultural, historical, and spiritual values of the community.
- Crests and Lineages: Totem poles often display crests, which are ancestral emblems that symbolize a particular clan or family lineage. These crests depict a specific animal, supernatural being, or natural element associated with the clan's history and identity. Totem poles serve as a visual representation of the clan's connection to their ancestral lands, their heritage, and their social structure.
- Storytelling and Oral Tradition: Totem poles are storytelling devices, conveying narratives and legends through their intricate carvings. Each figure on the totem pole contributes to a larger narrative, often passed down through generations orally. The stories depicted on the totem poles may include origin stories, historical events, heroic deeds, or teachings. These narratives preserve cultural knowledge,

reinforce community bonds, and ensure the continuity of Native traditions.
- Carving Techniques and Artists: Totem pole carving is a highly skilled art form that requires expertise, patience, and an understanding of cultural protocols. Native artisans, often working within family or community workshops, employ traditional techniques and tools to shape the wood into intricate forms. Carving a totem pole is a collaborative process, involving multiple carvers, each contributing their expertise to bring the design to life.
- Preservation and Revitalization Efforts: In recent years, there have been concerted efforts to preserve and revitalize the art of totem pole carving. Native communities and artists actively engage in cultural revitalization programs to pass down the knowledge and skills associated with totem pole carving to younger generations. These initiatives ensure the continuity of this ancient art form, safeguarding the cultural heritage of Alaska's indigenous peoples.

By delving into the history and symbolism of totem poles, we gain a deeper appreciation for the intricate craftsmanship and cultural significance of these remarkable structures. Totem poles serve as powerful reminders of the resilience, creativity, and spiritual connection of Alaska's Native communities. Through their striking imagery and storytelling, totem poles preserve and convey the diverse cultural traditions, values, and ancestral wisdom that continue to thrive in Alaska today..

Carving Techniques: Gaining an appreciation for the intricate craftsmanship and carving techniques used to create towering totem poles allows us to recognize the skill and dedication required to bring these works of art to life. The process of transforming massive cedar logs into stunning totem poles involves a combination of traditional tools, careful planning, and meticulous carving. Let's explore the fascinating world of totem pole craftsmanship and the techniques employed in their creation:

- Material Selection: Totem poles are primarily carved from cedar logs, specifically Western red cedar, which is abundant in the Pacific Northwest region. Cedar is chosen for its durability, workability, and resistance to decay. Selecting the right cedar log is crucial, considering factors such as size, quality, and suitability for the intended design.
- Design and Planning: Before carving begins, extensive design and planning are undertaken. This stage involves consultation with community members, clan leaders, and elders to determine the purpose, themes, and symbolism of the totem pole. Designs are sketched and refined, ensuring the incorporation of cultural narratives, clan crests, and meaningful symbols.
- Log Preparation: Once the design is finalized, the selected cedar log is carefully prepared for carving. The log is stripped of its bark and seasoned to reduce moisture content, making it easier to work with and minimizing the risk of splitting or warping. The log's dimensions are measured and marked to guide the carving process.

- Carving Tools: Traditional carving tools are used to shape the cedar log into a totem pole. These tools include adzes, chisels, gouges, and knives. The adze, a curved-blade tool, is particularly important for removing large sections of wood and shaping the general form of the totem pole. Smaller carving tools are then employed for detailed work, refining the intricate designs and symbols.
- Carving Techniques: Carvers employ a range of techniques to shape the wood and bring the totem pole to life. They use the adze to remove excess wood, creating the basic outline and contours. Fine detailing and intricate designs are achieved through gouging, chiseling, and carving with smaller tools. The carver must possess a keen eye for proportions, balance, and the integration of multiple figures within the design.
- Finishing and Preservation: After the main carving is complete, the totem pole undergoes finishing processes to enhance its appearance and protect it from the elements. This may involve sanding, smoothing the surface, and applying protective coatings such as varnish or natural oils. Preservation techniques are employed to safeguard the totem pole against insects, rot, and weathering, ensuring its longevity.
- Erecting and Installation: Once the totem pole is completed, it is ready for installation. Erecting a totem pole is a significant community event that involves a collaborative effort. The totem pole is carefully transported to its intended location, where it is securely mounted using various methods such as wedging or metal brackets. The raising of the totem

pole is accompanied by ceremonies, dances, and community celebrations, marking the completion of the artistic and cultural endeavor.

The craftsmanship and carving techniques used in creating totem poles demonstrate the deep connection between the artist, the material, and the cultural narratives they represent. The careful selection of materials, the meticulous planning, and the skillful use of traditional tools contribute to the stunning beauty and enduring presence of these monumental works of art. By appreciating the intricate craftsmanship involved, we gain a deeper understanding of the cultural significance and artistic excellence exemplified by totem poles.

Totem Pole Parks and Heritage Sites: Embarking on a journey to discover the awe-inspiring totem pole parks and heritage sites scattered across Alaska opens up a world of cultural exploration and the opportunity to witness the grandeur of these monumental sculptures up close. As you venture through the state, several notable locations stand out, each offering a unique glimpse into the rich history and artistic legacy of totem poles. Let's delve into some of these remarkable sites:

- Saxman Village: Located just outside Ketchikan, Saxman Village is renowned for its collection of intricately carved totem poles. This Tlingit community welcomes visitors to immerse themselves in the rich Native culture and witness the artistry firsthand. Stroll through the Totem Park, where numerous totem poles stand proudly, showcasing the

storytelling traditions and ancestral heritage of the Tlingit people.
- Totem Bight State Historical Park: Situated near Ketchikan, Totem Bight State Historical Park presents a captivating display of beautifully carved totem poles. The park features a recreated Native village, offering visitors a chance to step back in time and experience the cultural landscape of Alaska's indigenous communities. Explore the walking trails and marvel at the towering totem poles, which reveal the history and legends of the area's indigenous peoples.
- Totem Heritage Center: Located in Ketchikan, the Totem Heritage Center serves as a cultural repository, preserving and displaying historic totem poles rescued from abandoned Native villages. This center provides an invaluable opportunity to witness the restoration and conservation efforts undertaken to safeguard these remarkable works of art. Gain insights into the cultural significance of totem poles and the ongoing commitment to preserving Alaska's indigenous heritage.
- Sitka National Historical Park: Nestled in the coastal town of Sitka, Sitka National Historical Park is a captivating destination where nature and culture converge. The park is home to a collection of original and replica totem poles, each telling stories of the Tlingit people and their ancestral connections to the land. Take a leisurely walk along the Totem Trail, surrounded by lush forests and totemic artworks, while learning about the rich cultural traditions of the area.

- Alaska Native Heritage Center: Located in Anchorage, the Alaska Native Heritage Center is an immersive cultural center that showcases the diverse indigenous cultures of Alaska. The center features a captivating collection of totem poles from various Native groups, allowing visitors to appreciate the unique styles, designs, and symbolism associated with each region. Engage in interactive exhibits, traditional dance performances, and storytelling sessions to gain a deeper understanding of Alaska's rich Native heritage.
- Cape Fox Village: Situated in the town of Ketchikan, Cape Fox Village offers a glimpse into the cultural traditions of the Cape Fox Tlingit community. Explore the totem pole park, where meticulously crafted totem poles stand proudly amidst the beautiful natural surroundings. Marvel at the artistry and symbolism conveyed through these monumental sculptures, and learn about the history and legacy of the Cape Fox people.

Visiting these totem pole parks and heritage sites in Alaska provides a profound appreciation for the artistic mastery, cultural significance, and historical narratives represented by these towering works of art. It is a chance to witness firsthand the indelible connection between Alaska's indigenous communities, their land, and the enduring legacy of their cultural heritage. Through exploration and immersion in these remarkable locations, you will deepen your understanding of the rich tapestry of traditions and stories encapsulated within Alaska's totem pole heritage.

Contemporary Totem Pole Art: Exploring the evolution of totem pole art takes us on a captivating journey that spans generations and showcases the dynamic nature of Native artistic expression. From traditional designs rooted in ancestral traditions to the emergence of contemporary interpretations, the world of totem pole art continues to evolve, with modern Native artists pushing boundaries and infusing their work with unique perspectives. Let's delve into this fascinating evolution and discover the rich tapestry of totem pole artistry:

- Traditional Designs and Symbolism: Traditional totem pole art is deeply rooted in the cultural traditions and spiritual beliefs of Alaska's indigenous peoples. These designs often feature ancestral figures, animals, and mythical creatures, each symbolizing specific cultural narratives and teachings. Traditional totem poles serve as a visual language, communicating the stories, clan histories, and social structures of Native communities.
- Preservation and Revitalization: Over the years, efforts have been made to preserve and revitalize the art of totem pole carving. Elders, master carvers, and cultural organizations have played a crucial role in passing down the knowledge and techniques associated with traditional designs. This preservation ensures that ancestral traditions and craftsmanship are upheld, providing a strong foundation for contemporary artistic expressions.
- Cultural Continuity and Innovation: While honoring ancestral traditions, modern Native artists have embraced innovation and introduced contemporary

elements into their totem pole art. They explore new materials, techniques, and themes to create thought-provoking and visually captivating works. These artists infuse their unique perspectives, personal experiences, and socio-political commentary into their totem poles, offering fresh insights into the evolving cultural landscape.

- Cultural Collaboration: Many modern totem pole artists engage in collaborative projects that bring together multiple artistic voices and cultural perspectives. This collaboration fosters a rich exchange of ideas, techniques, and aesthetics, resulting in totem poles that blend diverse artistic influences and highlight the interconnectedness of indigenous communities.
- Environmental and Social Commentary: Contemporary totem pole art often addresses pressing environmental and social issues, reflecting the concerns and challenges faced by Native communities today. Artists incorporate symbols and imagery that convey messages about climate change, land preservation, cultural identity, and social justice. These totem poles serve as powerful statements, engaging viewers in critical conversations and encouraging a deeper understanding of contemporary indigenous experiences.
- Public Installations and Exhibitions: Modern totem pole art has gained recognition beyond cultural centers and museums, with public installations and exhibitions showcasing these innovative creations. Artists collaborate with communities, institutions, and public spaces to bring totem poles into urban

settings, parks, and prominent locations. These installations serve as a reminder of the enduring cultural presence of Alaska's indigenous peoples and invite dialogue between diverse audiences.

Exploring the evolution of totem pole art reveals the dynamic nature of Native artistic expression, where traditional designs intertwine with contemporary perspectives. Modern Native artists have embraced innovation while remaining deeply connected to their ancestral traditions, infusing their totem poles with personal narratives, social commentary, and environmental awareness. Through their artistic vision, these artists contribute to the preservation of cultural heritage, the celebration of indigenous identity, and the ongoing evolution of totem pole art as a vibrant and relevant form of artistic expression.

7.3 Alaskan Cuisine: Seafood Delights and Local Flavors

Alaska's pristine waters and bountiful wilderness provide the foundation for a remarkable culinary experience. In this chapter, we embark on a journey through Alaskan cuisine, celebrating its seafood delights, local flavors, and unique culinary traditions.

Seafood Bounty: Diving into Alaska's seafood bounty is a culinary adventure that unveils a world of exquisite flavors and a commitment to sustainable fishing practices. The state's pristine waters are teeming with an abundance of seafood, including succulent salmon, delectable halibut, flavorful Dungeness crab, and sweet spot prawns. Let's explore the remarkable seafood offerings of Alaska and discover the sustainable practices that preserve the freshness and quality of these prized delicacies:

- Salmon: Alaska is renowned for its world-class salmon, with five species that journey through its rivers and coastal waters. From the rich and buttery King salmon to the delicate and mild-flavored Sockeye salmon, each species offers a distinct culinary experience. Alaska's sustainable fishing practices include carefully managed salmon fisheries that prioritize responsible harvesting techniques, such as sustainable fishing quotas, habitat protection, and the use of selective fishing gear to minimize bycatch.
- Halibut: Another celebrated seafood gem of Alaska is halibut, prized for its firm and succulent flesh. Alaska's halibut fisheries are closely monitored and regulated to ensure the long-term sustainability of this valuable species. Responsible fishing methods, such as hook-and-line fishing, are employed to minimize the impact on the ecosystem and maintain the pristine quality of the catch.
- Dungeness Crab: Alaska's cold, nutrient-rich waters are home to the delectable Dungeness crab, known for its sweet and tender meat. Sustainable crab fisheries in Alaska prioritize the protection of breeding grounds and the implementation of size and catch limits. This ensures the long-term viability of the crab population and maintains the high quality and flavor of these delectable crustaceans.
- Spot Prawns: Alaska spot prawns are highly sought after for their delicate flavor and firm texture. Sustainable fishing practices for spot prawns involve

using traps that allow smaller prawns to escape, ensuring the reproductive capacity of the population. By adhering to size and catch limits, fishermen in Alaska maintain the health of the spot prawn population and guarantee a sustainable supply of these delectable crustaceans.
- Traceability and Quality Assurance: Alaska takes pride in its seafood traceability and quality assurance programs. Through strict regulations, comprehensive monitoring, and robust quality control measures, Alaska ensures that its seafood products meet the highest standards of freshness, taste, and safety. This commitment to quality assurance allows consumers to enjoy Alaska's seafood bounty with confidence, knowing that it is sustainably sourced and held to rigorous standards.
- Support for Local Communities: Alaska's sustainable fishing practices not only preserve the environment but also support the livelihoods and cultural heritage of local fishing communities. By prioritizing responsible fishing methods, Alaska ensures the long-term viability of the seafood industry, contributing to the economic stability and cultural resilience of coastal communities.

Indigenous Food Traditions: Discovering the traditional foodways of Alaska's Native peoples unveils a culinary tapestry deeply rooted in the land and sea. For centuries, Alaska's indigenous communities have relied on the bountiful resources of wild game, berries, and plants to create a cuisine that reflects their ingenuity, resourcefulness, and profound connection to the natural world. Let's delve into the traditional dishes that showcase the rich flavors and cultural significance of Alaska's Native cuisine:

Smoked Salmon: Smoked salmon holds a central place in Alaska's Native cuisine. Native communities have long practiced the art of smoking salmon, preserving this prized fish for the winter months. By carefully curing and smoking the fish over alder wood, they create a delicacy with a distinctive smoky flavor and a tender, moist texture. Smoked salmon is not only a flavorful dish but also a symbol of sustenance and cultural heritage.

- Akutaq (Eskimo Ice Cream): Akutaq, also known as Eskimo ice cream, is a unique and beloved dish in Alaska's Native cuisine. Traditionally made by blending whipped animal fat (such as seal or caribou), berries, and sometimes fish, this creamy and tangy dessert is a testament to the resourcefulness of indigenous cooking. Akutaq comes in various flavors, depending on the available ingredients, including wild berries like blueberries, cranberries, and cloudberries, providing a taste of Alaska's wild landscapes.
- Indian Fry Bread: Indian fry bread is a staple in many Native American cuisines, including Alaska's Native communities. This versatile bread is made by frying a simple dough made from flour, water, salt, and leavening agents. The result is a golden and crispy bread that can be enjoyed on its own, topped with savory ingredients like ground meat and vegetables, or drizzled with honey or powdered sugar for a sweet treat. Indian fry bread is a delicious embodiment of

Native ingenuity and adaptability in creating nourishing meals.
- Berries and Wild Plants: Alaska's Native cuisine celebrates the abundance of wild berries and plants found in the region. From blueberries and salmonberries to cloudberries and lingonberries, these vibrant and flavorful berries are used in a variety of dishes. They are incorporated into jams, desserts, and savory sauces, adding a burst of natural sweetness and acidity. Native communities also gather wild plants like beach greens, fireweed shoots, and fiddlehead ferns, incorporating them into salads, soups, and stews, infusing dishes with a unique and earthy taste.
- Fermented and Preserved Foods: Native communities have long practiced food preservation techniques to ensure a year-round food supply. Fermentation and preservation methods, such as fermenting fish (like black cod or herring), pickling vegetables, and drying meat, allow for the preservation of perishable ingredients and the development of complex flavors. These preserved foods not only sustain communities during harsh winters but also provide a glimpse into the cultural heritage and resourcefulness of Alaska's indigenous peoples.
- Traditional Hunting and Gathering: Alaska's Native cuisine is deeply intertwined with traditional hunting and gathering practices. Native communities rely on sustainable hunting and fishing methods to procure game such as moose, caribou, bear, and waterfowl. These meats are often incorporated into stews, soups,

and roasted dishes, providing nourishment and a deep connection to ancestral traditions.
- **Fusion of Cultures**: Experience the fusion of cultures that has shaped Alaska's culinary landscape. From Russian influences seen in dishes like borscht and pelmeni to Asian flavors brought by immigrants, such as sushi and stir-fried reindeer, Alaska's cuisine is a melting pot of diverse tastes and traditions.

Local Ingredients and Foraging: Learning about the abundance of wild ingredients that thrive in Alaska's pristine wilderness opens up a world of culinary exploration and highlights the deep connection between the land and its people. Alaska's vast and diverse ecosystems provide a fertile ground for a variety of wild mushrooms, berries, and edible plants that have been foraged and incorporated into both traditional and contemporary Alaskan dishes. Let's dive into the realm of wild ingredients and discover how they contribute to the unique flavors and experiences of Alaskan cuisine:

- Wild Mushrooms: Alaska's forests are teeming with a rich assortment of wild mushrooms, including morels, chanterelles, boletes, and porcini. Foraging for wild mushrooms has become a beloved activity for both locals and visitors, as these fungi offer unique flavors and textures. The art of mushroom foraging requires knowledge and expertise to identify the edible varieties and distinguish them from potentially toxic species. Once gathered, wild mushrooms find their way into a variety of Alaskan dishes, such as creamy

mushroom soups, sautéed mushroom side dishes, and flavorful mushroom sauces.
- Berries: Alaska boasts an incredible array of wild berries that thrive in its pristine landscapes. From the tart and vibrant cranberries and lingonberries to the sweet and juicy blueberries, salmonberries, and cloudberries, these berries are treasured ingredients in Alaskan cuisine. They are incorporated into jams, jellies, pies, desserts, and sauces, adding bursts of flavor, vivid colors, and natural sweetness. Many Alaskans partake in berry-picking excursions during the summer months, reveling in the joy of harvesting these wild treasures.
- Edible Plants: Alaska's wilderness is also home to a variety of edible plants that have been utilized by indigenous communities for centuries. From fireweed shoots, beach greens, and wild watercress to spruce tips and birch sap, these plants offer unique flavors and nutritional benefits. Contemporary Alaskan chefs and culinary enthusiasts have embraced the utilization of these edible plants, incorporating them into salads, soups, stir-fries, and infusions. The result is a celebration of the region's natural diversity and a deep connection to the land.
- Contemporary Culinary Innovation: Alaska's wild ingredients not only find their place in traditional dishes but also inspire contemporary culinary innovation. Chefs and home cooks alike experiment with these natural treasures, infusing them into modern interpretations of Alaskan cuisine. Wild ingredients may be incorporated into innovative cocktails, artisanal ice creams, infused oils and

vinegars, and savory dishes that showcase the unique flavors and textures of the region.
- Sustainable Practices and Ecosystem Stewardship: Foraging for wild ingredients in Alaska is closely tied to sustainable practices and ecosystem stewardship. Responsible foraging ensures the preservation of natural habitats and the continued abundance of wild ingredients. Ethical foragers understand the importance of not overharvesting and leaving behind a healthy ecosystem for future generations to enjoy.
- Cultural Heritage and Connection to the Land: Foraging for wild ingredients in Alaska is more than just a culinary pursuit—it is a way to connect with the land and honor the cultural heritage of indigenous communities. Many traditional practices and knowledge about wild ingredients have been passed down through generations, embodying a deep respect for nature and the wisdom of ancestral traditions.

By delving into the world of wild ingredients in Alaska, you embark on a sensory journey that celebrates the natural abundance, flavors, and cultural heritage of the region. The act of foraging not only connects you with the land and its offerings but also fosters a deeper appreciation for sustainable practices, biodiversity, and the delicate balance between humans and nature. Whether enjoyed in traditional dishes or innovative culinary creations, the incorporation of wild mushrooms, berries, and edible plants adds a touch of adventure, authenticity, and the untamed beauty of Alaska's wilderness to the plate.

Craft Brewing and Distilling: Embarking on a journey through Alaska's emerging craft brewing and distilling scene promises a delightful exploration of the region's unique flavors and innovative libations. As the craft beer and spirits movement takes hold in the Last Frontier, local breweries and distilleries are making their mark by harnessing the natural abundance of Alaska's ingredients and infusing them into their creations. Here's a taste of what awaits as you delve into Alaska's craft beverage scene:

- Craft Beers and Ales: Alaska's craft breweries are renowned for their inventive brews, incorporating local ingredients to create beers and ales that embody the spirit of the region. From the crisp and refreshing notes of spruce tip-infused pale ales to the malty richness of beers brewed with birch sap, these unique flavors pay homage to Alaska's wilderness. Craft brewers embrace the rugged landscape, infusing their creations with a touch of the untamed. Each sip offers a distinct taste experience that tells a story of the land.
- Spruce Tip Beers: Spruce tips, harvested from the new growth of spruce trees, contribute a distinct flavor profile to beers. These bright green tips infuse brews with citrusy, resinous, and slightly piney notes, creating a refreshing and aromatic beverage. Craft breweries in Alaska often incorporate locally sourced spruce tips into their seasonal releases, showcasing the distinctive taste of the region.
- Birch Sap Creations: Alaska's birch trees offer more than just their towering beauty. Craft brewers and distillers tap into the birch sap, which flows during the spring, to create unique and earthy flavors in their

libations. Birch sap beers and ales boast a subtle sweetness and a hint of floral and woody notes, providing a distinctive taste experience that transports you to the heart of Alaska's forests.
- Artisanal Spirits: Alaska's craft distilleries are also making waves with their artisanal spirits that celebrate the region's indigenous ingredients and flavors. Distillers embrace the bounty of the land, incorporating botanicals, berries, and herbs into their creations. You can savor spirits infused with local juniper berries, fireweed honey, or even Alaskan-grown grains, each offering a unique and authentic taste of the region.
- Tasting Flights and Brewery Tours: When exploring Alaska's craft beverage scene, it's a treat to indulge in tasting flights and brewery tours. Many breweries and distilleries open their doors to visitors, offering guided tours that take you behind the scenes of the brewing and distilling processes. You can witness the passion and craftsmanship firsthand, learn about the ingredients used, and experience the artistry of the brewing and distilling techniques. Tasting flights allow you to sample a range of beers, ales, and spirits, discovering the nuances and flavors that set them apart.
- Community and Local Flavors: Alaska's craft beverage scene fosters a sense of community and pride, with breweries and distilleries often collaborating with local farmers, foragers, and artisans. By sourcing ingredients from nearby farms and incorporating native botanicals, they showcase the flavors and character of the region. This commitment to

supporting local producers and embracing Alaska's natural resources creates a vibrant and interconnected ecosystem within the craft beverage industry.

Immersing yourself in Alaska's craft brewing and distilling scene unveils a world of flavors and craftsmanship that reflects the rugged beauty and distinctiveness of the region. With every sip, you not only taste the artistry and innovation of local brewers and distillers but also connect with the spirit of Alaska, where nature's abundance and creative passion combine to create truly memorable libations..

Culinary Experiences:

When it comes to culinary experiences in Alaska, there is an abundance of options that will tantalize your taste buds and immerse you in the region's vibrant food culture. From waterfront seafood restaurants to seafood festivals and cooking classes, Alaska offers a diverse array of culinary adventures. Here's a glimpse into the culinary experiences that await you:

- Waterfront Seafood Restaurants: Alaska's coastal location makes it a seafood lover's paradise. Picture yourself dining at waterfront restaurants, where you can relish the freshest catch of the day. From succulent salmon and buttery halibut to plump Dungeness crab and sweet spot prawns, these seafood establishments serve up delectable dishes that highlight the natural flavors of Alaskan seafood. As you savor each bite, you'll feel a connection to the ocean and appreciate the dedication of local

fishermen who bring these treasures from the sea to your plate.
- Seafood Festivals: Alaska's seafood festivals are a celebration of the region's bountiful harvest and culinary traditions. These events bring together locals and visitors alike, offering a vibrant atmosphere where you can indulge in a variety of seafood delights. From crab and shrimp feasts to salmon bakes and oyster shucking contests, these festivals showcase the diverse flavors and preparations of Alaskan seafood. Immerse yourself in the festivities, mingle with the locals, and experience the communal spirit that surrounds the love for seafood in Alaska.
- Cooking Classes: If you want to delve deeper into the secrets of Alaskan cuisine, participating in cooking classes is a fantastic way to do so. Local chefs and culinary experts guide you through the process of preparing traditional Alaskan dishes, sharing their knowledge and techniques. You'll have the opportunity to learn how to properly handle and cook seafood, discover the delicate balance of flavors in Alaskan recipes, and gain insights into the culinary heritage of the region. These interactive classes not only provide hands-on experience but also foster an appreciation for the importance of sustainable and locally sourced ingredients.
- Farm-to-Table Movement: Alaska's farm-to-table movement has gained momentum, with an increasing number of restaurants and establishments focusing on utilizing locally sourced ingredients. Explore restaurants that prioritize working directly with local farmers, foragers, and artisans to create dishes that

reflect the unique flavors and seasonal offerings of the region. This commitment to supporting local producers ensures that you experience the freshest ingredients while reducing the ecological footprint associated with long-distance food transportation.

- Sustainable and Locally Sourced Ingredients: Alaska's commitment to sustainability is reflected in its culinary scene. Many chefs and restaurant owners prioritize using sustainable and locally sourced ingredients, such as wild-caught seafood, organic vegetables, and free-range meats. By embracing these practices, they not only contribute to the preservation of the region's natural resources but also offer diners a chance to experience the true flavors of Alaska. This emphasis on sustainability and supporting local producers adds an extra layer of appreciation to every bite.
- Culinary Innovation: Alongside traditional Alaskan cuisine, the culinary scene in Alaska is also evolving with innovative interpretations and modern techniques. Chefs are incorporating global influences and experimenting with fusion cuisine, blending traditional Alaskan flavors with international culinary trends. This fusion of tradition and innovation results in exciting and unexpected flavor combinations that showcase the creativity and adaptability of Alaska's culinary scene.

Traditional Alaskan Recipes: Embarking on a culinary adventure through Alaska wouldn't be complete without discovering and mastering traditional Alaskan recipes. These recipes reflect the rich heritage and flavors of the region, showcasing the bounty of the land and sea. Whether you're a seasoned home cook or a culinary enthusiast, trying your hand at these traditional Alaskan recipes allows you to bring a taste of Alaska into your own kitchen. Here are a few iconic recipes to ignite your culinary creativity:

- Grilled Salmon with Maple Glaze: Alaska is renowned for its wild salmon, and grilling it with a sweet and tangy maple glaze is a classic preparation that highlights the natural flavors of this prized fish. The rich and flaky salmon, infused with smoky notes from the grill, perfectly complements the caramelized maple glaze. This recipe captures the essence of Alaska's wild salmon and offers a delightful balance of sweet and savory.
- Reindeer Sausage and Cabbage Stew: Reindeer meat is a treasured ingredient in Alaska and is often featured in hearty stews. A reindeer sausage and cabbage stew brings together the robust flavors of reindeer meat with the comforting qualities of cabbage, potatoes, and aromatic herbs. This nourishing and flavorful stew provides a taste of Alaska's wilderness and the sustenance it offers.
- Alaskan King Crab Legs with Garlic Butter: Alaskan king crab is a true delicacy, known for its succulent and sweet meat. Indulge in the simplicity and decadence of Alaskan king crab legs steamed or boiled to perfection, and served with melted garlic butter. The tender, juicy meat, paired with the rich and aromatic butter, creates a luxurious dining experience that epitomizes the best of Alaskan seafood.

- Eskimo Ice Cream (Akutaq): Akutaq, also known as Eskimo ice cream, is a traditional Alaskan dessert that showcases the resourcefulness of indigenous cooking. This unique concoction combines reindeer fat (or shortening), berries, sugar, and sometimes fish, resulting in a creamy and slightly tangy frozen treat. Akutaq offers a taste of Alaskan wilderness, with the sweetness of the berries and the richness of the fat or shortening blending harmoniously.
- Smoked Salmon Dip: Smoked salmon is a staple in Alaskan cuisine, and a smoked salmon dip is a crowd-pleasing appetizer that showcases the versatility of this flavorful fish. Combining smoked salmon with cream cheese, herbs, lemon juice, and spices creates a creamy and tangy dip that pairs perfectly with crackers or crusty bread. This recipe allows you to savor the essence of Alaskan smoked salmon in a simple and delicious way.

As you embark on your culinary exploration of Alaska, don't be afraid to experiment and put your own twist on these traditional recipes. Incorporate local ingredients, infuse them with your favorite flavors, and make them your own. The joy of cooking traditional Alaskan recipes lies in the opportunity to savor the flavors of Alaska and share them with family and friends, no matter where you are in the world. So, roll up your sleeves, gather your ingredients, and let the flavors of Alaska transport you to this captivating and delicious part of the world.

Whether you're a seafood lover, an adventurous foodie, or simply curious about the intersection of culture and cuisine, exploring Alaskan cuisine will provide a mouthwatering journey that reflects the unique flavors and culinary heritage of the Last Frontier.

CHAPTER EIGHT

Shore Excursions and Activities

8.1 Kayaking and Canoeing Adventures

Alaska's pristine waters offer a playground of adventure for kayaking and canoeing enthusiasts. With its vast coastline, fjords, and calm bays, this magnificent region provides an unparalleled opportunity to explore breathtaking landscapes and encounter abundant wildlife. Whether you're a beginner or an experienced paddler, Alaska's stunning waterways cater to all skill levels, making it an ideal destination for a memorable kayaking or canoeing adventure.

Imagine gliding through serene waters, surrounded by towering mountains, ancient glaciers, and lush forests. As you navigate along the coastline, hidden coves, remote islands, and secluded beaches await your discovery. The sense of freedom and tranquility that accompanies paddling through Alaska's pristine environments is truly unmatched.

One of the most remarkable aspects of kayaking and canoeing in Alaska is the chance to encounter its incredible wildlife. Keep a watchful eye for playful seals as they poke their heads above the water, curious sea otters frolicking among kelp forests, and majestic whales breaching the surface. The opportunity to witness these magnificent creatures in their natural habitat is a humbling and awe-inspiring experience.

Kayaking and canoeing tours in Alaska often provide knowledgeable guides who possess a deep understanding of the local marine ecology and geography. These guides are passionate about sharing their expertise and enriching your experience with fascinating insights into the region's natural wonders. From explaining the behavior of marine mammals to pointing out the diverse bird species that call Alaska home, these experts enhance your journey, making it an educational and engaging adventure.

For beginners, guided kayaking and canoeing tours offer a safe and structured introduction to the sport. Expert instructors will provide you with the necessary equipment, including the kayak or canoe, paddles, and safety gear. They will also give you a comprehensive briefing on paddling techniques, safety protocols, and navigation basics. This ensures that even if you have little to no experience, you can embark on your Alaskan kayaking or canoeing adventure with confidence.

For experienced paddlers, Alaska's vast waterways present a thrilling challenge. You can choose from a range of options, including multi-day expeditions, where you can fully immerse yourself in the untamed beauty of this wilderness. These extended journeys allow you to camp along the coastline, waking up to breathtaking sunrises and exploring remote areas inaccessible by other means.

Whether you prefer a guided tour or independent exploration, Alaska offers a multitude of kayaking and canoeing routes to suit your preferences. The Inside Passage, a renowned marine highway, is a popular choice for many kayakers. This scenic route stretches along the southeastern coast of Alaska, providing opportunities to explore majestic fjords, glacial valleys, and hidden waterfalls. Paddling through the Inside Passage allows you to witness the grandeur of Alaska's coastal landscapes up close.

Another popular kayaking destination is Glacier Bay National Park, a UNESCO World Heritage site. This vast wilderness is home to magnificent tidewater glaciers, dense rainforests, and an incredible diversity of marine and terrestrial wildlife. Kayaking in Glacier Bay offers an extraordinary chance to navigate through icy waters, surrounded by towering glaciers and snow-capped peaks.

For those seeking a truly remote and untouched experience, the Kenai Fjords National Park offers unparalleled beauty. Paddle along the rugged coastline, marveling at the sight of massive glaciers calving into the sea. Encounter sea lions basking on rocky outcrops, sea birds soaring above, and if you're lucky, spot the occasional pod of orcas gracefully gliding through the waters.

When planning your kayaking or canoeing adventure in Alaska, it is important to consider the weather and time of year. The summer months, particularly June through September, offer the most favorable conditions for paddling. The days are longer, the temperatures are milder, and the wildlife is more active. However, it's crucial to be prepared for the unpredictability of Alaskan weather. Sudden changes in wind patterns and the potential for fog or rain are common, so it's essential to dress in layers and carry proper rain gear to ensure your comfort and safety throughout your journey.

Before embarking on your kayaking or canoeing adventure, familiarize yourself with the Leave No Trace principles. These guidelines promote responsible outdoor ethics, ensuring that you minimize your impact on the environment and preserve the pristine nature of Alaska's waterways. Respect the wildlife and their habitats, dispose of waste properly, and be mindful of your surroundings to ensure the continued conservation of this remarkable ecosystem.

If you prefer a more immersive experience, consider camping along the coastline during your kayaking or canoeing expedition. Many areas in Alaska allow camping, providing an opportunity to truly connect with the natural environment. Wake up to the gentle sound of waves lapping against the shore, breathe in the crisp morning air, and enjoy the serenity of the wilderness around you.

In addition to kayaking and canoeing, Alaska offers a wealth of other activities to complement your adventure. Combine your paddling experience with hiking excursions, where you can explore the untamed wilderness on foot. Trek through ancient forests, encounter wildlife along the trails, and be rewarded with breathtaking vistas of rugged mountains and pristine lakes.

Helicopter tours are another thrilling way to enhance your Alaskan adventure. Soar above the vast landscapes, granting you a bird's-eye view of towering glaciers, cascading waterfalls, and remote valleys. Land in otherwise inaccessible locations and embark on guided hikes, immersing yourself in the heart of Alaska's untouched beauty.

If fishing is your passion, Alaska's waters are teeming with opportunities. Cast your line in pristine rivers and lakes, known for their abundance of salmon, trout, and halibut. Join a fishing trip or charter a boat to experience the thrill of reeling in a prized catch while surrounded by stunning natural scenery.

For a unique and authentic Alaskan experience, consider embarking on a crabbing excursion. Venture out to sea on a crabbing vessel, where you can actively participate in setting and retrieving crab pots. Learn from local experts about the art of crabbing and gain an appreciation for the hard work that goes into the industry. Indulge in the freshest and most succulent crab you'll ever taste as you savor the fruits of your labor.

To add a touch of adventure to your Alaska journey, immerse yourself in the world of dog sledding. This iconic Alaskan activity allows you to join a team of spirited and well-trained sled dogs as they whisk you across snow-covered trails. Learn about the history and traditions of dog sledding in Alaska, and gain a deep appreciation for the bond between musher and dog. Feel the rush of the sled gliding across the snowy landscape as you experience a timeless mode of transportation.

For the more adventurous souls, glacier trekking provides a once-in-a-lifetime opportunity to explore the mesmerizing world of ancient ice. Strap on crampons and venture onto the surface of a glacier, accompanied by experienced guides who ensure your safety and provide valuable insights into the unique glacial environment. Traverse deep crevasses, marvel at the vibrant blue hues of the ice, and witness the awe-inspiring power of these frozen giants.

Alaska's kayaking and canoeing adventures offer a blend of serenity, excitement, and exploration. The vast wilderness, pristine waters, and abundant wildlife create an unforgettable backdrop for your journey. Whether you choose to paddle through fjords, along the Inside Passage, or in the presence of glaciers, you'll be captivated by the raw beauty of this untamed landscape.

As you glide through Alaska's pristine waters, surrounded by breathtaking landscapes and abundant wildlife, you'll be reminded of the sheer magnificence of nature. The tranquility of the calm bays and coastal waterways creates a sense of peace and harmony, allowing you to disconnect from the stresses of everyday life and immerse yourself in the beauty of the natural world.

Kayaking and canoeing in Alaska offer a unique perspective on the region's geography and ecology. As you paddle along the coastline, you'll have the opportunity to explore hidden coves, remote islands, and secluded beaches that are inaccessible by other means of transportation. These hidden gems reveal the true essence of Alaska's coastal beauty, allowing you to appreciate the unspoiled landscapes and experience a sense of solitude that is rare to find in today's world.

The wildlife encounters during your kayaking or canoeing adventure are sure to leave an indelible mark on your memory. Alaska is home to a diverse array of marine and terrestrial species, and the waters along the coastline are teeming with life. Keep a watchful eye as you paddle, and you may be rewarded with sightings of playful seals basking in the sun, curious sea otters frolicking among kelp forests, or even the majestic breach of a humpback whale. These up-close encounters with wildlife offer a glimpse into their natural behaviors and create lifelong memories that will be cherished forever.

One of the most valuable aspects of joining a guided kayaking or canoeing tour is the opportunity to learn from experienced guides who possess an intimate knowledge of Alaska's marine ecology and geography. These guides are passionate about sharing their love for the region and are eager to provide you with fascinating insights into the local ecosystem. They can identify the various bird species that call Alaska home, explain the intricacies of marine food chains, and shed light on the geological forces that have shaped the coastline over millions of years. By the end of your journey, you'll not only have paddled through Alaska's stunning waterways but also gained a deeper understanding and appreciation for its natural wonders.

For beginners, kayaking or canoeing in Alaska offers an accessible and enjoyable way to engage with the outdoors. Guided tours cater to all skill levels, providing instruction on paddling techniques, safety protocols, and navigation skills. Even if you've never been in a kayak or canoe before, you'll feel confident and comfortable under the guidance of experienced instructors who prioritize your safety and enjoyment.

Experienced paddlers will find Alaska to be a paradise for adventure. The vastness of the coastline and the diversity of waterways present a plethora of options for exploration. From leisurely day trips to multi-day expeditions, there is something to suit every paddler's desire for challenge and discovery. As you venture farther into Alaska's remote areas, you'll find yourself in awe of the untouched wilderness that surrounds you, with opportunities to camp under the stars and wake up to the sounds of nature in its purest form.

When preparing for your kayaking or canoeing adventure in Alaska, it's important to consider the unique weather conditions and plan accordingly. Alaska is known for its rapidly changing weather patterns, so packing appropriate clothing and gear is essential. Dressing in layers will allow you to adapt to temperature fluctuations throughout the day, and investing in quality rain gear will ensure you stay dry during unexpected showers. Additionally, bringing sunscreen, insect repellent, and a sturdy hat will protect you from the elements and enhance your overall comfort.

While kayaking and canoeing in Alaska offer a thrilling and unforgettable experience, it's crucial to prioritize safety at all times. Always wear a personal flotation device (PFD) and ensure it is properly fitted. Familiarize yourself with basic rescue techniques and emergency procedures, and be mindful of your surroundings and the potential hazards of the water. It's also wise to check weather forecasts and tidal conditions before setting out on your journey to ensure that you are aware of any potential risks or changes in conditions.

In conclusion, Alaska's pristine waters beckon kayaking and canoeing enthusiasts with their awe-inspiring beauty and abundant wildlife. Whether you're a beginner seeking a peaceful exploration of hidden coves and remote islands or an experienced paddler craving the thrill of venturing into untouched wilderness, Alaska offers a myriad of opportunities to satisfy your adventurous spirit. Guided tours provide knowledgeable guides who enrich your experience with their expertise, sharing insights into the region's ecology and geography. As you glide through the calm bays and coastal waterways, surrounded by breathtaking landscapes and the wonders of nature, you'll create memories that will last a lifetime. So, grab your paddle, embrace the serenity, and embark on an unforgettable kayaking or canoeing adventure in the magnificent wilderness of Alaska.

8.2 Hiking and Helicopter Tours

Alaska's rugged terrain and diverse ecosystems create a hiker's paradise, where every step unveils stunning vistas, ancient forests, and alpine meadows. Whether you're a casual stroller or an experienced mountaineer, Alaska offers a multitude of hiking trails that cater to all skill levels and preferences, ensuring an unforgettable adventure in the heart of nature.

The options for hiking in Alaska are as diverse as the landscapes themselves. For those seeking a short and scenic walk, there are numerous trails that wind through picturesque valleys, along crystal-clear streams, and past vibrant wildflower meadows. These trails offer a taste of Alaska's beauty without requiring extensive time or physical exertion, making them accessible to hikers of all ages and fitness levels. You might find yourself wandering through the serene Denali National Park, where gentle trails lead you to panoramic viewpoints that showcase the majesty of North America's highest peak, Denali (formerly known as Mount McKinley).

For the more adventurous hikers, Alaska presents a plethora of challenging trails that test your endurance and reward you with awe-inspiring panoramas. As you ascend steep mountain slopes and traverse rugged terrain, you'll be surrounded by dramatic landscapes that seem straight out of a postcard. One such iconic trail is the rigorous but rewarding Kesugi Ridge Trail in Denali State Park. This multi-day trek offers sweeping views of the Alaska Range, with glaciers, lakes, and alpine tundra stretching as far as the eye can see.

Alaska's national parks are a treasure trove for hiking enthusiasts. Wrangell-St. Elias National Park, the largest national park in the United States, is a paradise for adventurers. With its vast expanse of untamed wilderness, the park boasts an extensive network of trails that lead to breathtaking glaciers, deep canyons, and towering peaks. Hike along the Root Glacier Trail, where you can strap on crampons and explore the mesmerizing blue ice formations up close. Or challenge yourself on the historic Chilkoot Trail, retracing the footsteps of gold rush stampeders as you traverse challenging terrain and learn about the rich history of the region.

Helicopter tours offer a unique and exhilarating way to experience Alaska's remote and inaccessible landscapes. Soar above the rugged mountains, cascading glaciers, and vast icefields, reveling in the unparalleled beauty that unfolds beneath you. These awe-inspiring aerial perspectives provide a true sense of the scale and grandeur of Alaska's wilderness. As the helicopter lands in remote and pristine locations, you have the opportunity to step foot in areas that are otherwise inaccessible, allowing you to embark on guided hikes that immerse you in the heart of untouched nature.

Imagine standing on a remote alpine ridge, surrounded by jagged peaks and endless expanses of untouched wilderness. The air is crisp, and the only sounds you hear are the gentle rustling of the wind and the distant calls of wildlife. Guided hikes during helicopter tours offer a unique chance to explore these pristine environments, with knowledgeable guides leading the way and sharing their expertise on the natural and cultural history of the area. From spotting rare alpine flowers to marveling at the remnants of ancient glaciers, these hikes offer a deeper understanding and appreciation of the delicate ecosystems that thrive in Alaska's remote corners.

One popular destination for helicopter-assisted hikes is the vast and untamed Alaska Range. With its jagged peaks and sweeping glaciers, this mountain range is a playground for adventurers. Helicopter tours take you deep into this alpine paradise, where you can embark on unforgettable hikes that lead you through valleys carpeted with wildflowers, along ridges with panoramic views, and up to high alpine passes where you can witness the raw power of nature. The opportunities for exploration are endless, and each step brings you closer to the heart of Alaska's untamed wilderness.

The advantages of helicopter-assisted hikes are not limited to the stunning scenery and remote access they provide. These tours also offer a unique perspective on the interconnectedness of Alaska's ecosystems. From the air, you can witness the intricate web of rivers, lakes, and wetlands that sustain a rich variety of wildlife. As you touch down and embark on your guided hike, your knowledgeable guide will point out the flora and fauna that call this pristine environment home. Keep an eye out for grizzly bears foraging in the meadows, moose grazing along the riverbanks, and bald eagles soaring above the treetops. These encounters with Alaska's iconic wildlife add an extra layer of excitement and appreciation to your hiking experience.

As with any outdoor adventure, safety should be a top priority when embarking on hiking or helicopter tours in Alaska. The wilderness can be unpredictable, and weather conditions can change rapidly. It is essential to come prepared with proper clothing, sturdy footwear, and essential gear such as maps, compasses, and first aid kits. Be sure to check weather forecasts and trail conditions before setting out, and inform someone of your hiking plans in case of emergencies. Respect any guidelines or restrictions in place to protect the environment and wildlife, and always practice Leave No Trace principles to ensure the preservation of Alaska's pristine landscapes for future generations.

Beyond the physical challenges and breathtaking landscapes, hiking and helicopter tours in Alaska offer a profound connection with nature. The vastness of the wilderness and the solitude found along the trails provide a unique opportunity for self-reflection and introspection. The absence of distractions allows you to fully immerse yourself in the beauty of the natural world, fostering a sense of peace and serenity that is increasingly rare in our fast-paced lives.

Whether you choose to explore Alaska's trails on foot or embark on a helicopter-assisted hike, you are guaranteed an unforgettable adventure. The raw and untamed beauty of Alaska's rugged terrain will leave an indelible mark on your soul. From the majesty of its mountains to the awe-inspiring power of its glaciers, Alaska beckons you to embrace its wild side and discover the wonders that await around every bend in the trail or from the vantage point of a helicopter. So, put on your hiking boots, embrace the spirit of exploration, and embark on an extraordinary journey through Alaska's breathtaking landscapes.

8.3 Fishing Trips and Crabbing Excursions

Alaska's reputation as a premier fishing destination is well-deserved, as its waters are teeming with an abundance of fish species that attract anglers from near and far. Whether you're a seasoned angler with years of experience or a beginner eager to cast your first line, Alaska offers a wide range of fishing trips and experiences that cater to all skill levels and interests.

One of the most popular fishing experiences in Alaska is freshwater fishing. The state is home to countless rivers, streams, and lakes that are rich in salmon, trout, and other prized game fish. From the mighty Kenai River, famous for its world-class salmon runs, to the tranquil streams nestled in remote wilderness areas, there is no shortage of opportunities to reel in a trophy catch. Salmon fishing in Alaska is a thrilling adventure, with five species of Pacific salmon (king, silver, sockeye, chum, and pink) making their annual migrations from the ocean to their spawning grounds in the state's rivers. Hooking into a powerful salmon and feeling the exhilarating fight is an experience that anglers cherish for a lifetime. Trout fishing is equally rewarding, with Alaska's rivers and lakes offering ample opportunities to catch native rainbow trout, Dolly Varden, and Arctic grayling. Whether you prefer fly fishing or spin casting, Alaska's freshwater fishing will captivate you with its beauty and bounty.

For those seeking a different kind of fishing adventure, Alaska's coastal waters offer an abundance of opportunities to catch halibut, rockfish, and other marine species. Halibut fishing is particularly popular, as these enormous flatfish can grow to impressive sizes, providing anglers with an exhilarating challenge. Charter boats depart from coastal towns and take you to prime fishing grounds, where you'll drop your line and wait for that telltale tug. Reeling in a massive halibut from the depths of the ocean is an adrenaline-pumping experience that will test your strength and skill. Additionally, Alaska's coastal waters are home to a variety of rockfish species, including the colorful and coveted yelloweye rockfish. These fish not only provide an exciting fishing experience but are also delicious table fare, adding a culinary delight to your Alaskan fishing adventure.

If you're looking for a unique Alaskan experience that goes beyond traditional fishing, consider joining a crabbing excursion. Alaska is famous for its succulent king crab and other delectable crab species, and participating in a crabbing trip allows you to get up close and personal with this iconic seafood. Step aboard a crabbing vessel and venture out to sea, where you'll learn the art of crabbing from local experts. Help set and retrieve crab pots, feeling the anticipation build as you pull up the traps to reveal the bounty within. As you immerse yourself in the process, you'll gain an appreciation for the hard work and skill required to catch these delectable crustaceans. And the best part? You get to savor the rewards firsthand as you indulge in the freshest and most flavorful crab onboard. It's a truly interactive and delicious adventure that showcases Alaska's abundant marine bounty.

Fishing trips and crabbing excursions in Alaska not only provide thrilling angling opportunities but also allow you to immerse yourself in the state's natural beauty and learn about its rich marine ecosystem. Knowledgeable guides accompany you on these excursions, sharing their expertise on fishing techniques, local fish species, and the importance of sustainable fishing practices. They are passionate about conservation and ensuring the long-term health of Alaska's fisheries, providing valuable insights on catch-and-release practices, bag limits, and other responsible fishing guidelines. Engaging with these guides allows you to deepen your understanding of the delicate balance between human interaction and the preservation of Alaska's marine resources.

When planning a fishing trip or crabbing excursion in Alaska, there are a few important considerations to keep in mind. First and foremost, it's essential to research and choose a reputable fishing charter or tour operator. Look for companies with experienced guides, positive reviews, and a commitment to sustainable fishing practices. These operators will not only maximize your chances of a successful fishing experience but also ensure that you're fishing within legal limits and protecting the environment.

Next, consider the timing of your trip. Different fish species have specific seasons and peak times for fishing. For example, salmon runs typically occur during the summer months, while halibut fishing is best from May to September. Research the optimal times for the species you're targeting to increase your chances of a successful and rewarding fishing experience.

Additionally, it's important to pack the right gear and equipment for your fishing adventure. Depending on the type of fishing you plan to do, you may need to bring your own fishing rod, reel, tackle, and appropriate clothing. If you're participating in a guided fishing trip, the outfitter will often provide the necessary equipment, but it's always a good idea to check in advance and ensure you have everything you need for a comfortable and enjoyable fishing experience.

Lastly, be prepared for the weather conditions you may encounter during your fishing trip. Alaska's climate can be unpredictable, so it's wise to dress in layers and bring rain gear, sunscreen, insect repellent, and any other essentials to keep you comfortable throughout the day. It's also advisable to check the weather forecast before heading out and be prepared for potential changes in conditions.

Whether you're casting your line in a serene river, battling a powerful halibut in the open ocean, or participating in a thrilling crabbing excursion, fishing in Alaska offers an unparalleled experience for anglers of all levels. The state's pristine waters and diverse fish populations create an angler's paradise, where the thrill of the catch is enhanced by the breathtaking beauty of the surroundings. So, pack your fishing gear, embrace the spirit of adventure, and set sail for an unforgettable fishing journey in the majestic waters of Alaska.

8.4 Dog Sledding and Glacier Trekking

Dog sledding and glacier trekking are two exhilarating activities that allow you to immerse yourself in the raw beauty and rich history of Alaska's wilderness. These experiences provide a unique perspective on the region's cultural heritage and its awe-inspiring natural wonders.

Dog sledding, also known as mushing, has deep roots in Alaska's history and is deeply intertwined with the state's identity. Step into the world of mushing as you join a team of spirited and well-trained sled dogs on a thrilling adventure through snow-covered trails. The bond between musher and dogs is truly remarkable, and you'll witness the unwavering teamwork and dedication of these incredible canines as they pull you along the pristine landscapes.

As you glide through the snowy terrain, your senses will come alive. The crisp mountain air, the sound of paws rhythmically hitting the snow, and the sight of the majestic Alaskan wilderness stretching out before you create an unforgettable experience. Imagine racing through boreal forests, across frozen lakes, and up snow-covered hills, with the sheer power and agility of the dogs propelling you forward. The exhilaration of dog sledding is unmatched, as you become one with the natural surroundings and tap into the age-old tradition of traversing Alaska's winter wonderland.

Dog sledding is not just a thrilling adventure; it's also an opportunity to delve into the history and cultural significance of this traditional Alaskan mode of transportation. The practice of dog sledding has been essential for Alaskan communities for centuries, serving as a means of transportation, communication, and survival in the harsh winter conditions. On your dog sledding excursion, you'll learn about the fascinating history of mushing and gain insights into the unique bond between musher and sled dog. Professional guides and mushers are often passionate storytellers, sharing tales of legendary races like the Iditarod and Yukon Quest, as well as personal anecdotes that highlight the profound connection between humans and their canine companions.

Glacier trekking, on the other hand, offers an entirely different adventure that takes you into the heart of Alaska's ancient ice formations. Strap on crampons and join professional guides as you explore the stunning world of glaciers. These immense rivers of ice, formed over thousands of years, offer a glimpse into the raw power and beauty of nature.

As you navigate across the glacier's surface, you'll witness breathtaking scenes that seem like they belong in another world. Deep crevasses, towering ice walls, and mesmerizing ice sculptures will captivate your senses and leave you in awe of nature's grandeur. The vibrant blue hues of the ice create a surreal atmosphere, evoking a sense of wonder and enchantment. Professional guides are well-versed in glacial safety and provide the necessary equipment and knowledge to ensure your adventure is both thrilling and safe.

Glacier trekking allows you to experience the unique characteristics of these frozen landscapes up close. With each step, you'll gain a deeper appreciation for the fragility and resilience of these icy giants. Your guides will share their expertise, explaining the formation of glaciers, their importance in shaping the landscape, and the effects of climate change on these delicate ecosystems. It's an opportunity to learn about the intricate interplay between ice, water, and the surrounding environment.

Safety is paramount when venturing onto glaciers, as their constantly shifting nature requires expertise and caution. The guides accompanying you on your trek are experienced professionals who prioritize your well-being and provide valuable insights into glacial safety protocols. They are well-versed in glacier dynamics, weather patterns, and rescue techniques, ensuring that you can fully immerse yourself in the experience with confidence.

Both dog sledding and glacier trekking offer unique perspectives on Alaska's natural wonders and cultural heritage. They provide opportunities to engage with the environment, learn aboutthe history and traditions of Alaska, and create lasting memories of adventure and exploration.

When planning a dog sledding or glacier trekking excursion in Alaska, it's important to consider a few key factors. First and foremost, choose a reputable tour operator or guide service that prioritizes safety, sustainability, and responsible tourism practices. Look for companies that have experienced guides, well-cared-for sled dogs, and a commitment to minimizing their impact on the environment.

For dog sledding, it's essential to ensure that the dogs are treated with care and respect. Look for operators that prioritize the well-being of their sled dogs, providing proper training, nutrition, and veterinary care. Responsible operators also limit the number of passengers per sled to ensure the dogs' welfare and optimize the experience for all participants.

When it comes to glacier trekking, be prepared for the physical demands of the activity. Glacier surfaces can be uneven and icy, requiring good balance and strength. It's advisable to have a moderate level of fitness and consult with your tour operator about any physical requirements or limitations. Dress in layers to accommodate changing temperatures and wear sturdy, waterproof footwear that can accommodate crampons.

Throughout your dog sledding or glacier trekking adventure, take the time to appreciate the unique environment around you. The beauty of Alaska's winter landscapes, whether it's the pristine snow-covered trails or the awe-inspiring glacial formations, is best experienced with a sense of mindfulness and appreciation. Embrace the opportunity to disconnect from the modern world and immerse yourself in the tranquility and serenity of the Alaskan wilderness.

As you embark on these adventures, remember that preservation and conservation are crucial. The Alaskan wilderness is fragile and should be treated with respect. Follow Leave No Trace principles, dispose of waste properly, and minimize your impact on the environment. By practicing responsible tourism, you contribute to the long-term preservation of Alaska's natural treasures for future generations to enjoy.

Dog sledding and glacier trekking in Alaska are not merely recreational activities; they are transformative experiences that connect you with the spirit of the land and its people. From the rich history of dog sledding to the awe-inspiring beauty of glacial landscapes, these adventures allow you to forge a deep and lasting connection with the natural wonders of Alaska. So, embrace the thrill, embrace the beauty, and embark on a journey that will leave you with memories to cherish for a lifetime.

Embarking on these exhilarating activities in Alaska guarantees unforgettable moments, allowing you to immerse yourself in the raw beauty and adventure that this magnificent region has to offer.

CHAPTER NINE

Tips for Maximizing Your Alaska Cruise Experience

9.1 Capturing the Perfect Photos and Videos

When cruising through the magnificent landscapes of Alaska, you'll be surrounded by awe-inspiring vistas, majestic wildlife, and breathtaking glaciers. The desire to capture these incredible moments through photography and videography is only natural. By following a few tips and techniques, you can ensure that you capture the perfect photos and videos that will forever preserve the memories of your Alaskan adventure.

Bring the Right Equipment

To capture stunning images, it's important to have the right equipment. Consider carrying a DSLR camera with interchangeable lenses or a high-quality smartphone with a good camera. Both options offer excellent capabilities for capturing Alaskan landscapes and wildlife. Don't forget to pack extra batteries, memory cards, and any necessary accessories such as a tripod, filters, or a waterproof casing if you plan to shoot in challenging environments.

Research Photography Techniques

Familiarize yourself with basic photography techniques to make the most of your equipment. Understanding concepts such as composition, lighting, and exposure will greatly improve the quality of your photos. Composition involves arranging the elements in your frame to create visually appealing images. Learn about the rule of thirds, leading lines, and symmetry to compose your shots effectively. Experiment with different angles and perspectives to capture unique and captivating images that showcase the grandeur of Alaska.

Consider the lighting conditions and how they affect your subject. Take advantage of Alaska's long daylight hours, particularly during the summer months, to capture the soft golden light during sunrise and sunset. These times of the day often provide the most magical and warm illumination for your photographs. Additionally, pay attention to the direction and quality of light to create depth and enhance textures in your images.

Capture Wildlife Moments

Alaska is renowned for its diverse and abundant wildlife. From breaching whales to soaring eagles and bears catching salmon, there are countless opportunities to capture these magnificent creatures in their natural habitats. To increase your chances of capturing wildlife moments, be patient and observant. Keep your camera ready and set to an appropriate shooting mode for action shots. Telephoto lenses or zoom capabilities on your camera will allow you to capture wildlife from a safe distance without disturbing their natural behavior.

Use burst mode or continuous shooting to capture a sequence of images, increasing the likelihood of capturing the perfect shot in a dynamic wildlife situation. Remember to respect wildlife and observe them from a safe distance. Never approach or disturb them for the sake of a photograph. Be mindful of any guidelines or instructions provided by naturalist guides or park rangers to ensure the well-being of both the animals and yourself.

Utilize Natural Lighting

Alaska's unique geography and long daylight hours offer incredible opportunities for capturing photos in natural light. The soft and warm light during sunrise and sunset, known as the "golden hour," creates a magical atmosphere and enhances the beauty of the landscapes. Plan your photography outings around these times to take advantage of the captivating colors and dramatic lighting conditions. Experiment with different angles and compositions to make the most of the golden hour and create stunning images that showcase the beauty of Alaska.

During midday when the sunlight is harsh and shadows are strong, consider focusing on close-up details or capturing landscapes with strong graphic elements. Experiment with backlighting to create silhouettes or use fill flash to balance the exposure in challenging lighting conditions. Remember to adjust your camera settings accordingly to achieve the desired exposure and preserve the details in highlights and shadows.

Use the Environment Creatively

Alaska's landscapes are truly awe-inspiring, with towering mountains, sparkling glaciers, and serene fjords. When composing your shots, use the environment creatively to add depth and context to your images. Incorporate elements such as glaciers, mountains, or fjords as backdrops to create visually captivating compositions. Pay attention to leading lines in the landscape that can guide the viewer's eyes through the frame. Utilize foreground elementssuch as rocks, flowers, or trees to create a sense of scale and depth in your photographs. These elements will help tell a more complete story of the Alaskan environment and enhance the impact of your images.

Experiment with different perspectives and angles to capture unique views of the landscapes. Try shooting from low angles to emphasize the grandeur of the mountains or get down to ground level to showcase the intricate details of wildflowers or moss-covered rocks. Look for reflections in calm waters or use the movement of waves to create dynamic compositions. By exploring different creative approaches, you can capture images that stand out and truly convey the beauty of Alaska.

Take Advantage of Onboard Photography Workshops

Many cruise lines that offer Alaska cruises provide onboard photography workshops conducted by professional photographers. These workshops offer a fantastic opportunity to enhance your skills, learn new techniques, and gain insights from experts in the field. Attend these sessions to sharpen your photography knowledge and receive personalized guidance on capturing the best photos and videos during your Alaskan journey. These workshops often cover various topics such as composition, exposure, wildlife photography, and post-processing. Take advantage of the expertise available onboard to improve your photography skills and make the most of your Alaskan cruise.

Remember, capturing great photos and videos in Alaska is not solely about the equipment or technical aspects of photography. It's about capturing the essence and beauty of Alaska's natural wonders. Take the time to immerse yourself in the environment, appreciate the breathtaking landscapes, and connect with the wildlife and local culture. By approaching your photography with passion and a deep appreciation for the natural world, you'll be able to create images that truly reflect the incredible experience of cruising through Alaska. Embrace the opportunity to tell a visual story of your Alaskan adventure and preserve the memories for years to come through your photographs and videos.

9.2 Onboard Entertainment and Enrichment Programs

While sailing through the pristine waters of Alaska on your cruise ship, you'll have the opportunity to indulge in a variety of onboard entertainment and enrichment programs. These activities are designed to enhance your voyage, providing a well-rounded and enriching experience. From live performances to educational lectures and hands-on workshops, here are some highlights to look forward to during your Alaska cruise:

Live Performances:

Prepare to be captivated by the talented performers who grace the stages of the cruise ship. From Broadway-style productions to intimate concerts, there's something for everyone. Enjoy the melodic tunes of musicians, be mesmerized by the graceful movements of dancers, and be entertained by comedians who will have you laughing out loud. These live performances add a touch of glamour and excitement to your evenings at sea.

Educational Lectures:

Immerse yourself in the rich history, culture, and natural wonders of Alaska through informative lectures delivered by experts. Learn about the geological formation of the region, the diverse wildlife that inhabits its lands and waters, and the significance of indigenous cultures. These lectures provide valuable insights into Alaska's unique ecosystem, helping you develop a deeper appreciation for the natural wonders you'll encounter during your journey.

Culinary Demonstrations:

Embark on a culinary adventure as you delve into the flavors of Alaska through interactive culinary demonstrations led by onboard chefs. Gain insights into the region's local ingredients, traditional cooking techniques, and signature dishes. Watch as skilled chefs prepare delectable creations right before your eyes and savor the opportunity to sample some of Alaska's gastronomic delights. These demonstrations are not only informative but also a treat for your taste buds.

Workshops and Classes:

Engage your creative side with a variety of hands-on workshops and classes offered onboard. Unleash your artistic talents in art classes where you can learn techniques such as painting or sketching. Hone your photography skills in workshops led by experienced photographers who will guide you in capturing the best shots of Alaska's breathtaking landscapes. Join mixology lessons to learn how to craft delicious cocktails or participate in dance classes to master some new moves. You can even try your hand at cooking lessons to expand your culinary repertoire. These interactive experiences allow you to learn something new, develop new skills, and have fun along the way.

Casino and Gaming Activities:

If you enjoy games of chance, cruise ships often have onboard casinos where you can try your luck. Step into the exciting world of gambling and enjoy a range of casino games, from slot machines to poker, blackjack, or roulette. Whether you're a seasoned player or trying your hand at gambling for the first time, the onboard casino offers an entertaining and vibrant atmosphere where you can test your luck and enjoy the thrill of gaming.

Movie Screenings and Theaters:

For those seeking relaxation and entertainment, the ship's theaters provide a haven of comfort and entertainment. Enjoy movie screenings where you can catch up on the latest blockbusters or classics, immersing yourself in a cinematic experience at sea. The theaters may also host live performances, ranging from music concerts to comedy shows or theatrical productions. These onboard theaters offer a fantastic opportunity to unwind, enjoy some downtime, and be transported into different worlds of entertainment.

Fitness and Wellness Activities:

Maintain your fitness routine while onboard by taking advantage of the ship's fitness facilities. Stay active with state-of-the-art gyms equipped with modern exercise machines and weights. Engage in group fitness classes led by professional instructors, offering a variety of options such as yoga, Pilates, aerobics, or spinning. Take a dip in the ship's swimming pools to refresh and invigorate your body. Sports courts are available for those seeking more active pursuits, where you can engage in friendly matches of basketball, tennis, or volleyball. Additionally, onboard wellness activities provide opportunities for relaxation and rejuvenation. Join yoga classes to find inner balance and harmony, participate in wellness seminars where you can learn about maintaining a healthy lifestyle, or indulge in spa treatments that offer ultimate pampering and tranquility. These fitness and wellness activities ensure that you can take care of your physical and mental well-being while enjoying your Alaskan cruise.

By participating in these onboard entertainment and enrichment programs, you'll have a well-rounded and enriching experience during your Alaska cruise. Whether you're seeking thrilling performances, educational insights, creative pursuits, or moments of relaxation, the cruise ship provides a plethora of options to cater to your interests and preferences. Embrace these activities as opportunities to immerse yourself in the onboard atmosphere, connect with fellow passengers, and create lasting memories of your Alaskan adventure.

9.3 Souvenir Shopping and Local Crafts

Alaska, with its rugged landscapes and rich cultural heritage, offers a treasure trove of souvenirs and local crafts that capture the essence of this remarkable destination. When exploring the ports of call during your Alaska cruise, set aside time for souvenir shopping to bring home a piece of Alaska's unique culture and natural beauty. Here are some popular items to consider:

Native Artwork and Crafts:

Alaska's indigenous cultures have a profound influence on the region, and you'll find a wide range of Native artwork and crafts that reflect their rich heritage. Look for intricate totem poles, hand-carved wooden sculptures, masks adorned with traditional designs, and beautifully woven baskets. Each piece tells a story and celebrates the diverse indigenous cultures of Alaska. These unique artworks not only make for exceptional souvenirs but also serve as meaningful reminders of the region's cultural legacy.

Jewelry and Accessories:

Alaska is renowned for its abundant natural resources, including precious gemstones and metals. Consider purchasing jewelry made with Alaskan gemstones like jade, gold nuggets, or fossilized walrus ivory. These pieces are often crafted into stunning necklaces, earrings, bracelets, and rings, featuring native-inspired designs that showcase the beauty of Alaska's natural elements. Owning a piece of Alaskan jewelry not only adds a touch of elegance to your wardrobe but also connects you to the region's geological wonders.

Local Food Products:

Alaska's bountiful waters provide some of the freshest and most delectable seafood in the world. Take the opportunity to bring home a taste of Alaska by purchasing local food products. Smoked salmon, Alaskan king crab legs, and jars of wild berry jams and preserves are popular choices. These culinary delights allow you to savor the flavors of Alaska long after your cruise, and they make excellent gifts for food enthusiasts back home. Immerse yourself in the rich culinary heritage of Alaska and indulge in these delicious treats.

Clothing and Apparel:

Stay warm and stylish while showcasing your love for Alaska with clothing and apparel inspired by the region. Look for fleece jackets adorned with wildlife motifs or iconic Alaskan landscapes. Keep cozy with hats and scarves featuring traditional designs or the iconic Northern Lights. T-shirts with images of bears, eagles, or Alaska's stunning glaciers are also popular choices. These clothing items not only provide practicality and comfort during your Alaska cruise but also serve as wearable mementos that celebrate your unforgettable journey.

Alaskan Souvenirs and Trinkets:

For small yet meaningful keepsakes, explore the wide range of Alaskan souvenirs and trinkets available in local shops. Magnets featuring Alaska's famous landmarks, keychains adorned with wildlife, postcards showcasing breathtaking landscapes, and ornaments representing native symbols are just a few examples. These small tokens serve as reminders of your Alaskan adventure and can be cherished as collectibles or shared as gifts with loved ones.

Art Galleries and Studios:

Immerse yourself in Alaska's vibrant art scene by visiting local art galleries and studios. Here, you'll find original paintings, sculptures, pottery, and other unique artistic creations crafted by talented Alaskan artists. The artworks often draw inspiration from the region's stunning landscapes, wildlife, and indigenous cultures. By acquiring a piece of Alaskan art, you not only support local artists but also bring home a truly one-of-a-kind piece that encapsulates the spirit of Alaska's artistry and creativity.

As you embark on your souvenir shopping adventure in Alaska, remember to seek out reputable shops that source their products ethically and support local artisans and communities. These practices ensure that your purchases contribute to the sustainability and preservation of Alaska's cultural and natural heritage. By choosing souvenirs that resonate with you personally and reflect the uniqueness of Alaska, you can carry apiece of this extraordinary destination with you and share its beauty and stories with others for years to come.

When purchasing souvenirs, consider supporting local artisans and businesses, that promote sustainable and ethical practices. Take the time to learn about the artists and craftsmen behind the products, as it adds a deeper connection to your chosen souvenirs.

9.4 Best Practices for Responsible Travel in Alaska

Alaska's pristine wilderness and delicate ecosystems are home to a diverse array of wildlife and natural wonders. As visitors, it is our responsibility to travel responsibly and minimize our impact on the environment. By following these best practices for responsible travel during your Alaska cruise, you can help preserve the region's natural beauty for generations to come:

Respect Wildlife:

Alaska is renowned for its incredible wildlife, including bears, whales, eagles, and more. When encountering wildlife, observe from a safe distance and never approach or feed animals. Keep noise levels low to avoid causing stress or disturbance to their natural behavior. Following these guidelines ensures that wildlife can thrive undisturbed and maintains the integrity of their habitats. Listen carefully to naturalist guides or park rangers who provide instructions on how to responsibly interact with wildlife during shore excursions or wildlife-watching activities.

Leave No Trace:

Alaska's wilderness is a pristine environment, and it's crucial to leave it as you found it. Dispose of trash properly and avoid littering. Carry a small bag to collect any waste generated during shore excursions or outdoor activities, and ensure that it is properly disposed of later. Avoid damaging plants, disturbing rocks, or removing artifacts. By practicing "Leave No Trace" principles, you help preserve the natural beauty of Alaska's landscapes and minimize your impact on the delicate ecosystems.

Support Local Communities:

When exploring Alaska's coastal towns, make a conscious effort to support local businesses. Patronize local restaurants, shops, and tour operators that are owned and operated by members of the community. This not only contributes to the local economy but also fosters sustainable tourism practices. By supporting local businesses, you directly contribute to the preservation of Alaska's unique cultural heritage and traditional ways of life.

Opt for Eco-Friendly Activities:

Choose tour operators and excursions that prioritize environmental sustainability and conservation. Look for eco-certifications or practices that minimize carbon emissions, waste generation, and ecological disruption. Opt for activities that have minimal impact on the environment, such as guided hikes, kayaking tours, or wildlife-watching excursions that adhere to responsible wildlife viewing guidelines. By selecting eco-friendly options, you actively support the preservation of Alaska's fragile ecosystems and help ensure their longevity for future generations.

Conserve Water and Energy:

Onboard the cruise ship, be mindful of your water and energy usage. Follow any guidelines provided by the cruise line to reduce your environmental footprint. Reuse towels and linens when possible, turn off lights and electrical appliances when not in use, and be conscious of your water consumption. These small actions can collectively make a significant difference in conserving resources and reducing the cruise ship's overall environmental impact.

Learn about Indigenous Cultures:

Take the time to learn about Alaska's indigenous cultures, traditions, and history. Respect cultural sites, artifacts, and sacred areas. Seek permission before entering culturally significant places or participating in cultural activities. Educate yourself about the rich heritage of Alaska's native peoples, their customs, and their relationship with the land. By understanding and appreciating their cultural significance, you show respect for their traditions and contribute to the preservation of their cultural heritage.

Support Conservation Efforts:

Consider supporting local conservation organizations by making donations or participating in volunteer programs. These organizations work tirelessly to protect Alaska's natural resources, conduct scientific research, restore habitats, and promote sustainable practices. Your contribution can help fund crucial conservation initiatives and ensure the long-term preservation of Alaska's unique ecosystems and wildlife.

By adopting these responsible travel practices, you become an ambassador for sustainable tourism in Alaska. Your conscious efforts to respect wildlife, minimize waste, support local communities, choose eco-friendly activities, conserve resources, appreciate indigenous cultures, and contribute to conservation efforts will contribute to the long-term sustainability of Alaska's natural wonders. Let's strive to leave a positive impact and ensure that future generations can continue to enjoy the pristine beauty of Alaska's remarkable landscapes and wildlife. Together, we can make a difference and protect this extraordinary destination for years to come.

CHAPTER TEN

Conclusion

10.1 Appendix: Basic Phrases and Vocabulary

As you embark on your Alaskan adventure, it can be helpful to familiarize yourself with some basic phrases and vocabulary to enhance your interactions with locals and navigate through the region. Here are a few essential phrases and words to assist you:

Greetings and Common Phrases:

- Hello: "Hello" or "Hi"
- Good morning: "Good morning"
- Good afternoon: "Good afternoon"
- Good evening: "Good evening"
- Thank you: "Thank you"
- Please: "Please"
- Excuse me: "Excuse me"
- Sorry: "Sorry"
- Yes: "Yes"
- No: "No"
- Goodbye: "Goodbye"
- Have a nice day: "Have a nice day"

Directions and Transportation:

- Where is...?: "Where is...?"

- How do I get to...?: "How do I get to...?"
- Can you help me?: "Can you help me?"
- Bus station: "Bus station"
- Train station: "Train station"
- Airport: "Airport"
- Taxi: "Taxi"
- Left: "Left"
- Right: "Right"
- Straight ahead: "Straight ahead"

Food and Drinks:

- Menu: "Menu"
- Water: "Water"
- Coffee: "Coffee"
- Tea: "Tea"
- Breakfast: "Breakfast"
- Lunch: "Lunch"
- Dinner: "Dinner"
- Vegetarian: "Vegetarian"
- Can I have the bill, please?: "Can I have the bill, please?"

Shopping and Souvenirs:

- How much does it cost?: "How much does it cost?"
- I would like to buy...: "I would like to buy..."
- Do you have...?: "Do you have...?"
- Souvenir: "Souvenir"
- Gift shop: "Gift shop"
- Cash or credit card?: "Cash or credit card?"

Emergencies:

- Help!: "Help!"
- I need a doctor: "I need a doctor"
- Police: "Police"
- Hospital: "Hospital"
- Fire: "Fire"
- Nature and Wildlife:
- Mountain: "Mountain"
- Glacier: "Glacier"
- Forest: "Forest"
- Wildlife: "Wildlife"
- Bear: "Bear"
- Moose: "Moose"
- Whale: "Whale"
- Eagle: "Eagle"
- Salmon: "Salmon"

Remember, these basic phrases and vocabulary can be a starting point for your Alaskan journey. Learning a few local words and expressions can go a long way in fostering connections, showing respect for the culture, and making your experience even more enjoyable.

Made in the USA
Columbia, SC
10 July 2024